I0058719

Building Your Dream

By: Matthew Brown

©2013

ISBN 978-0-9832593-9-8

<u>Dedication</u>

I'd like to first thank my wife for giving me the time to write this book. Business is something that I have always had a huge passion for and I found writing this book helped turn on those juices even more. I was finally able and willing to put down my own thoughts about how to create a successful business.

I would also like to thank my parents for teaching me more then I probably think I know. I learned a lot from watching others succeed and fail. There are always ups and downs in life and in business. Its knowing how to get back up and try again that was one of the most important lessons I was taught.

I would also like to thank my other friends and family that helped the process with ideas and editing the final version(s). So thank you all for your feedback and notes.

Thank you!

~ M.B.

Forward

Thank you for your interest first off. Whether you are a member of the family, friend, or just a total stranger. I hope you enjoy reading and I hope that you learn at least something from what I have written here.

Most of the information you find in this book is based on my personal opinion, which can be different then many other business minded people. Probably what I have conversations about the most with people is my chapter about breaking even from the start.

Business is one of the passions in my life and the area where I started and will probably end my career in some form or another. I have always been interested in business from the age of a young child and I get just as excited talking about business in any form with others people around me.

I truly hope you enjoy the book and feel free to contact me with any questions or comments if you have any. You can always find me through my consulting business at www.brownconsultingwork.com.

Enjoy the ride!

~ M.B.

Table of Contents

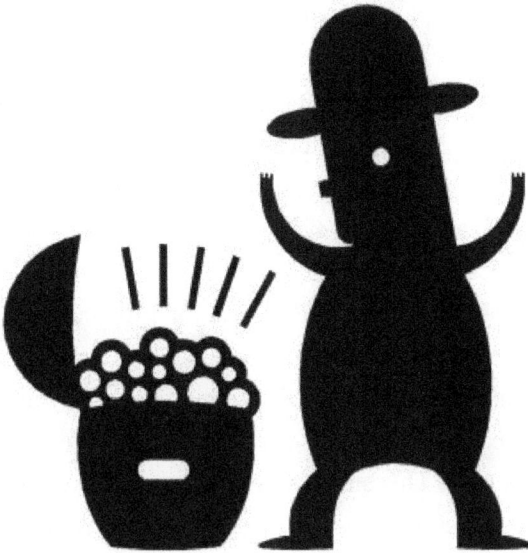

Lesson 1: The True American Dream; Greed

I am sure it has happened to all of us in the middle of the night or on our way to our full time normal jobs. For some, an idea can come out of nowhere when we are sitting on the couch watching a television program or sitting somewhere else doing something else that I don't need to discuss in a book because it has already been written. Taro Gomi calls it "Everyone Poops" and it can be purchased online for about six dollars on Amazon. We think of that great idea that would make us millions, right? That one idea that will save ourselves, pay off the debt we have incurred from living years of the "American Dream", which basically is to incur as much debt as possible and as many needless inanimate objects and possessions as possible.

That really was the "American Dream" in the 2000s. Just like a gallon of milk left in the fridge to long though, it did not take long for people to realize the bad odor and voluptuous lumpy curds exiting the bottle as we come downstairs for a midnight night peanut butter and jelly sandwich and a cold glass of milk to help wash everything down. What I mean is the payments that come along with having things like too much credit card debt, which essentially come from credit card companies that spend hundreds of millions of dollars to market their product to people that cannot even afford to make payments and some that likely do not even have a job. A house payment you cannot truly afford based on an income that you tend to over-estimate to lenders that never truly did a decent background check and did not even check on the length of your job that you just got because the lender is more concerned about seeing a commission check for selling you a house for $300,000 that is now worth about $160,000 or worse. Then of course we have to mention that brand new car payment that is probably a little high because you have rolled so much negative equity into your car that you are even upside down in your car loan as well. This stems as well to car dealerships that are more than happy to roll that negative equity over into a brand new car loan so you can purchase a brand new 2014 model instead of driving around that old 2013 model you just purchased about six months ago.

Do not let me get started on the wrong foot or interpretation though. I am not advocating that all of our problems are someone else's. It is not the car dealer's fault that you want to trade in your 2013 model to purchase a 2014 model. They are more than willing to help though. It is not the credit card lender's fault that you want to open up another credit card to make purchases you cannot truly afford. They are more than willing to help though. And I cannot blame them, only to a point though. A credit card company is a business just like everything else. A lending agency is just a business as well. A business's sole purpose is to make money. That is what they are doing. Whether we agree with their ethical behavior and how they run their business is an entirely different discussion for a later dinner party.

I think we can all agree that to some extent there are some things that we should not have been given over our time here. That third credit card was probably not really needed. If every one of us had a little "finance angel" sitting on our shoulder telling us what we should and should not do, would that have helped us come to an understanding that we did not need a third credit card? Should the credit card company be that financial angel telling us that we cannot have more than two credit cards and turning us down? If they did, that credit card company probably would not be in business because there are 10 other card companies right around the corner chomping at the bit to get your business (and your debt with interest).

In my personal opinion it would take an act of congress and probably much more to set strict limits on people incurring debt requirements & limits for such large purchases and acquisitions of debt. Now I know that is NEVER going to happen in America even though I think everyone could agree that something like that is needed and would help our country get back to a manageable personal debt level. Is it any surprise that the "normal" family household has about $10,000 just in credit card debt alone? That does not even include student loans, mortgages, and car payments.

Just imagine what could be possible. You are 18 years old and the only debt you are allowed to have is 2 outstanding debts. One would be a student loan for attending college if you needed it. The second debt would be a car loan (with requirements). What sort of requirements? Well you could start with something like a certain percentage down on the initial auto loan (which could be capped at $20,000 for example) and terms no longer then 60 months.

Now let us go one step further in purchasing a house. In the early 2000s and even at some places today, you can purchase a house with no money down. Some areas in the United States actually offer a zero-down house loan if you live "outside" a major city limit. My family took advantage of such a program when purchasing our first home. We live in the next town over to a larger city, which is really a two-minute drive. It is not like our city is not a real city; we have a police department and a Wal-Mart, so it is not like we are living out in the sticks and boonies.

Choosing to live outside a larger metropolis area saved us about $5,000-$10,000 in cash that we would have had to put down to get into a home. In the height of the housing market though, MANY people and companies took advantage of themselves and "loose" loan standards to say the least, which caused many families and people to get into home ownership before they were actually ready and before many could even really afford a mortgage payment. It is obvious now there were a lot of people to blame both companies and people on the outside as well. Just like most of our history in America though, history will tend to repeat itself again and again because we just cannot help ourselves to greed. Those that live through it, may learn lessons for the future, but newcomers and baby boomers will eventually make the same mistakes as our forefathers. I would not call it human nature, but how about "American Nature". I think that name fits pretty well. So let us wait and see what the next financial meltdown will look like. My educated guess would be anytime between 2020-2025.

Not a believer in history repeating itself? Lets take a brief history lesson shall we. For your sake and mine, I am just going to start in the 20th Century, but believe me that these re-occurrences of financial crisis occur well back into Napoleon's days.

Let us start with the Panic of 1907, otherwise known as the Knickerbocker Crisis. This crisis occurred when the New York Stock Exchange fell almost 50% from its peak in the prior year. When this happened everyone and their grandmother ran to the bank to pull out all their money and hide it the old fashioned way, in their mattress. Well this quickly spread across the US and before you could say Knickerbocker, local and state banks were entering bankruptcy because they had no money from customers to earn interest on. The reason for the name Knickerbocker Crisis was because the main culprit behind this crisis was the Knickerbocker Trust, which at the time was one of the largest banks in the US. The bank had a novel plan to try and drive up the cost of copper by cornering the marketing (owning enough of something like stock to influence the price). Their plan became public thanks to the National Bank of Commerce that found out and said they would no longer accept checks from the Knickerbocker Trust. Then everyone else followed suit and demanded their funds back from the Trust Company. The main person behind it committed suicide after seeking help from J.P. Morgan, but was turned away by J.P. Morgan. Shortly after that, the government enlisted the help of J.P. Morgan in which the company pledged a large sum of money and convinced others to do the same and invest back into the banking system. Although a dreadful situation, an interesting note for history buffs, the following years, Senator Nelson Aldrich, who was the father-in-law of John D Rockefeller Jr., chaired a commission to investigate this crisis and this led to the creation of the Federal Reserve System. The main purpose of the Federal Reserve System was to watch over things like this and make sure it never happens again. (uh... way to go guys). In a nutshell, the 1907 crisis = Greed.

Several years later, here we are in 1929 and the Great Depression, which lasted until about 1939ish. This is the crisis we all probably know about the best because we learned about it in history class or some people now may have actually lived through it. Although the Great Depression was not only in the US, but also worldwide, it is worth noting because of its magnitude. However do not get too excited as it did start in the United States on October 29th, 1929, known as Black Tuesday with another similar stock market crash.

Then we can skip ahead (skipping over a couple minor crisis, but nothing too major enough to write about) to the Savings and Loan Crisis of the 1980s and 1990s. In 1979, then chairman of the Federal Reserve, in an act to reduce inflation, doubled interest rates for the Savings and Loans associations in the United States. If you are unaware, a Savings and Loans Association is a financial institution that accepts savings deposits and makes car and mortgage loans as well as other personal loans to individuals. Making this change to interest rates though backfired and actually caused many banks (747 out of 3,234) fail because it was using short-term money to finance long term loans. What made it worse though is that to try and show things positively, many CEOs of these institutions used some "creative accounting" methods to make their business look more profitable, much similar to how a ponzi scheme works, where a new investors' money is used to pay off old/original investors (pretty much exactly what you see on every episode of American Greed if you watch that show on A&E). In a nutshell, 1980s & 1990s crisis = Greed.

Now you can fast-forward to 2006 when we just start to see the housing bubble start to slow down and then dramatically fall off a cliff faster then grandma in a wheel chair being shoved off the Grand Canyon because she cannot stop talking about "back in her days..." So where to begin on this crisis? Let us start at the most obvious point; greed. One major contributing factor could have been you. Were you one of the large numbers of new homeowners that could not afford to pay their mortgage when your low-introductory rate suddenly increased? If so, then you are partially to blame. Where did you think an adjustable rate mortgage was going; down? Let me tell you right here right now, your adjustable rate mortgage will NEVER go down. Its not a questions of whether it will go up, it is just a question of how high.

So, here is where we are now. You know that history will repeat itself and the question that remains is that are you prepared for that? Are you ready to start a business with the knowledge now that another crisis is a mere 10-20 years away? I am going to assume that the answer is yes, and you will continue reading. If not, I hope you have learned something from this first chapter and you can at least walk away a little smarter. But I must digress now; let us get back to why you are here. You came up with that one truly individual idea that will save yourself from all of this and hopefully you can personally prosper with a little greed for yourself. What do you do now? I'm glad you asked.

Lesson 2: The Idea

Ok, so now you have this great idea. What should you do first? Well the first thing you must do is research, research, and more research. Talk to as many people as you can and get their thoughts about your idea. Is your business a brick and mortar (actual store) or some sort of online business? Both require research on your part. If you are thinking of opening a brick and mortar store, I am sure you can understand why it may take you a little longer to put together a full idea as opposed to an internet business that could be started up fairly quickly and probably less expensive.

So take, at the very least, a full evening and start searching the Internet for ideas like yours. Trust me, no matter what you think of, someone has always thought of either exactly it or something very close to your idea. The Internet is a great tool these days to find information on pretty much anything you would like. Google is my favorite search engine, although there are many out there to choose from and each one has good and bad things about them.

Just because someone has come up with something similar or exactly what you thought of, does not mean you should give up. Hell no. If this is something you are passionate about, never give up on your dream otherwise you are going to be left with living in reality and just working your normal nine to five job just to pay your bills. Do not be discouraged when you find someone that is doing the same thing. Do new musicians get discouraged because they can never find a "new" chord? Heck, if you look at popular music during anytime you will find that the same chords may be used in a million different songs, but each one just has a little difference in tone and/or rhythm to make it unique for that particular song. Just because someone has come up with the same idea, do not give up.

This is your opportunity to take a new spin, a new rhythm, and a new tone on your idea to make it unique and stand out from all the rest of the other ideas out there. At the very least, you should be able to take a DEEP look into this other person's idea and figure out how you could improve on the same model, find the mistakes that they went through in starting their business and learn from them.

Learn everything you can from that business so you can apply the same great principals and not make the same mistakes that they did. Knowledge from experience is something that cannot be taught. We all remember our parents telling us what not to do and what we should be doing. They gave us advice when we did not want it and probably would not listen anyways. Yet, for some reason, they tend to always be right. I love the saying, "I wish I knew then what I know now". Just think of all the trials and tribulations you could have avoided had you listened to the advice that someone from an older generation gave you. Just like I mentioned earlier, our history tends to repeat itself and it is no different in our personal lives. Our children will make the same mistakes we did, just like our parents made mistakes that their parents made. It is the circle of life and for a strange reason that I do not even pretend to comprehend, as hard as we may try sometimes, we just cannot break the cycle of these mistakes.

Your idea may be as simple as having your own restaurant. That is great, but what kind of restaurant? Who are you catering your business for? Where would you like the restaurant to be located? These are the type of brainstorming questions you need to keep in mind, as you get ready to sit down and write your business plan. Yes, that is right, you need to write a business plan. Why you ask? Because no business has ever succeeded without at least some type of business plan. Start brainstorming ideas now how you are going to market your product, how you are going to sell your product, what type of business you want to own, how you are going to finance your idea, etc, etc. These are all important questions that you should be asking yourself as you sit down and brainstorm your idea and expand it into an outline of sorts. Once you have this brainstorming session complete, its time to get serious about looking at yourself in the mirror and asking... am I worthy? Would a bank honestly give me a loan to start this business? If you were an outsider looking in, would you give yourself the money to start this business? If the answer is no, which 90% of you out there should be saying that, read the next chapter on cleaning yourself up. If you are part of the minority (10%) that have their lives and finances together, you are welcome to skip Lesson 3, but do not be afraid of a little extra reading as it might not be a bad idea to brush up on your skills.

Lesson 3: Clean Yourself Up

I mean it in the most sincere manner, honestly. I cannot tell you how many people I see every day that take no pride in their appearance or the business's appearance. It really just boils down to laziness. Take your personal appearance for example. To me, this seems like something that everyone should have already figured out or been taught in the early stages of their lives, but for some reason, some people just have not connected the dots. These are the people still spending 20 minutes on a connect-the-dots game trying to figure out what the picture is. I think it is pretty sad that I have to at least mention to clean yourself up before starting your business, but I mean this in two very different ways.

The first way is hygiene. It is not rocket science to figure out to take a shower, comb your hair, brush your teeth, etc, etc. But still, some people still neglect these things and out in the real world, let me tell you something… we can see it… and smell it! It is pretty obvious when someone has not taken a shower or has chosen to be deodorant free from the weekend. When you are out looking at starting a business, looking for investors, looking for locations, talking to people, anything, how you look and act with your appearance and body language can make or break someone's interest and willingness to help you out.

The next few paragraphs here are directed at men particularly and how they should dress.

First, buy yourself at least 2 nice outfits. You don't have to buy a suit, but that would be best. You can get away these days with a nice pair of pants and a dress shirt. You do not have to be James Bond, unless you really want to. It will not hurt anything by any means. But showing an effort to keep up a better appearance starts off a good first impression.

Here's a walkthrough understanding of a basic wardrobe for men.
- 2 pairs of dress slacks that fit correctly (no baggy pants!). Those colors should be black and brown.
- 2 pairs of dress shoes. Those colors should be black and brown. Dress and casual style are what you should shoot for. Slip-on dress shoes are a good choice as you can dress those up or where them with a pair of khakis on the weekend. The bonus feature of never worrying about re-tying your shoelaces during the day is a nice thought to think of.
- 2 Button up dress shirts. These colors should be solid Blue and solid white. You can use these with any pant and shoe combination and you can dress it up with a tie, go casual with the sleeves rolled up, or just un-buttoned at the top.
- 1 or 2 belts. Again the colors should be black and brown. If you would rather buy a reversible belt so you have the best of both worlds in one that is ok too. ALWAYS MATCH YOUR BELT AND SHOES!!!
- Ditch the white socks and buy a pair of black and brown socks. Match them with your shoes. Nothing fancy, so just solid colors are needed, again in black and brown.

There you go gentlemen, a basic wardrobe to get you started at looking professional. Overtime you can add more pieces to your closet, but this section is just a basic "get-started" list for you. So let's talk about first impressions for a quick minute.

First rule about making a good first impression is to be on time to your meetings. This does not mean running in on the dot, but rather show up 5-10 minutes before you are suppose to be there. Try not to push longer then 10 minutes, as some people might get an impression that you have nothing better to do. If you arrive early, wait in your car and listen to the radio for a few minutes or go over your meeting thoughts. Take a few minutes to think about any specific questions (if you are starting your first business, you should have a laundry list of questions already going).

Be confident when talking, which means standing tall, making eye contact and giving a firm handshake. Small talk can go a long way with someone you are talking with. Do not be afraid to say you do not know something. If you are small talking with someone before the meeting and he or she mention something that you do not understand, ask them. It helps engage that person to remember you after you leave because you had a "personal" conversation with them and you showed an interest in something they were talking about. Probably one of the biggest turnoffs in an initial first impression is if your phone goes off. TURN OFF OR SILENCE YOUR CELL PHONE! If your phone goes off, don't immediately check it! It can wait till you are done with your meeting!

Its important to remember that a first impression only lasts about 5-10 seconds when you meet someone and unfortunately once that impression is made, it can take years in some cases to prove people wrong if they get the wrong first impression. Most of this should be common sense, but I believe it is worth being said, because someone out there may not know and be afraid to ask. So there you are.

Now lets talk about cleaning you up financially. How much debt do you have right now either by yourself or with your family? Do not be afraid, like I said earlier, most families these days carry about $10,000 worth of credit card debt along with everything else. It is nothing to be ashamed of, but its something you and your family have to recognize to be able to understand how to get out of it.

First thing you should do is pull your credit report. You can do this over the Internet by going to several websites, but I suggest going to one of the big three credit bureaus, which are Equifax, Experian, and TransUnion. All three of these companies have the ability to print off your credit report and send it to you over email or a quick download after answering a few questions. For example, I pull my credit score and report from Equifax once a year just to check things out and make sure there is no identity theft or funny things going on. Equifax makes you sign up for a monitoring service which will charge you $3-$4 per month for "constant monitoring". Unfortunately, you have to sign up for this to get your credit report for free, but just wait a few days after you get your report and then call them and cancel it before you even get your first month's charge.

I would suggest checking your credit score at least once a year these days just to be safe. I had never checked my credit report until my wife and I went to purchase our first home. We found out that someone had somehow got her SSN number and was opening up several accounts at a cell phone company in another state. When one account would close because of non-payment, they would just open another one. It took us personally about 4-5 months to straighten everything out with the cell company and get everything corrected on her credit report. If you do find something wrong or illegal on your credit report, there are services available to help you with these problems, but you will have to pay them most likely. If you decide to go this route, just make sure you choose a reliable and professional service. You can always check with your local credit union or banks to see if they know of any references.

Take a look at all your debt. If you do not have much, then you are in luck and it will most likely be a lot easier for you to try and get investors or financing for your business. In most cases however, the amount of debt you personally have can play a big part in getting approved or even looked at for financing of your business, especially a startup. Be well aware there are plenty of people and Internet sites out there that will tell you about grants and free financing for your business. 99.99% of them are all scams you will find eventually, and the other .01% that is actually real you most likely won't even get close to getting anything substantial. If it truly was real then there are 100x more people out there looking for start up funds just like you for their own bright idea.

It should be no surprise that the first place you should look is family for help. Most likely you have talked to your family by now about your idea and they may be able to give you a little help in financing your dream, or at least giving you a little something to put towards a down payment on financing through a normal institution. Cleaning up your credit will help a bank look at your seriously. A bank will not care about your business plan or your great aspirations to change the world. Like I said in chapter one, a bank is a business above anything else and their main purpose is to make money. They make money off the interest you are going to payback during your loan. They do not care how stupid or insane your idea is, they only care if you make on-time payments.

If you are looking down that road at getting a business loan, look at your credit report and figure out your debt-to-income ratio. This is just a fancy word for a simple formula. It is your recurring monthly debt (credit cards, mortgage, car loans) (nothing like water bills, groceries, etc.) divided by your gross monthly income. If you are at 35% or below, then you are in good shape and have a better chance at seriously looking into a small business loan. If you are above 35%, you need to look closer at your debt and figure out how to get below 35%, which is probably as simple as just putting an extra hundred or two hundred on the credit card each month.

Getting out of debt is about making priorities, not excuses. It can be easier if it is just you, because it is a lot easier to fight with yourself over expenses, as there is no one else to really blame except yourself. When you have a family situation, things can get more stressful since there are likely more hands in the cookie jar. If you are in this family situation, take a proactive approach in writing how much debt you have to pay off somewhere and crossing it off as you go along. Do not get bogged down at the giant number at the end of the road. It can be about smaller and baby steps. Taking things at a weekly or monthly goal instead of a final destination. If the debt you want to pay off is $15,000 that can be huge to look at every day. But if you break that down to pay off $150 extra each month, it can seem easier. If you have multiple credit cards, you may "feel" better crossing off the smallest card rather then the biggest first. Find what works best for you and keep pushing forward.

Some of the most successful people that I see get out of debt the fastest are the ones that make the choice to shred their credit cards and strictly use cash. Even the use of a debit card can be misleading at times because you never "see" the actual money. Having cash in your hand, knowing that a $20 bill must last you one pay period for lunches is a constant reminder of how you actually spend your money and what frivolous things we all buy throughout the day.

Another thing to do is look on the internet and brainstorm with people about things you can do around town for free instead of always having to go out and spend $30-$40 on seeing a movie Friday night or spending $50-$60 a night for a meal with the family out on the town. This can help keep you mind busy and thinking of things to do that do not have to cost you anything. Keep reaching for that goal and find a way to reward yourself every now and then. For example, let's say your goal was to pay off $5,000 in credit card debt over the course of a year. So you can simply break that down to see that in 6 months you should have about $2500 left. If you reach that goal, great! Find a way to treat yourself appropriately and within your budget.

Lesson 4: Working with Family & Friends

Now by this point you have probably talked to more then a few friends and family members about your idea. They have probably asked you a bunch of questions that have hopefully got you thinking about some facets of your business and business model. You have probably also got a few "I'd be interested in helping you out" or "Can I get in with you on that". So now we have to sit down and talk about getting involved with family and friends. The very simplest way to answer this question and end this chapter in the shortest manner would be just to say no to friends and family. That is what many professional business owners will probably tell you if you ask them. The reason for that is because, just like history, business owners tend to repeat themselves just the same, and continue to hire friends and family to help out in their business.

Lets start at one of the beginning steps of the business, which would be financing your business start-up. Many banks will tell you that it is the first place people go when starting their own business. They usually dig deep into their own pockets scrounging around any loose five cent pop can they can find (Yes, I said pop, not soda) and depending on how deep you dig, selling some of those prized processions that you so eagerly bought with your credit cards and never use anymore. You might likely be looking to sell that exercise bike and stair climber that you told your wife you would use every day and would help you get back in shape to the size of pants you used to wear in college before your metabolism slowed down to that of a turtle, you started losing some of your hair but have not told anyone yet because you are only 35 and why the hell am I losing hair at age 35!? Well eating McDonalds every day for lunch and grabbing a pop on your way to work probably does not help the aging process that well, so you really have no one else to blame except yourself. However, everything is going to be fine now because you have come up with this great business idea and you just need a little seed money to help get you started. This is the time when friends and family usually come into the picture and you start rationalizing the thought process of borrowing money from your parents or bringing on a partner and friend that seems to have some decent ideas and wants to get involved. So how do you want to handle it?

My uneducated guess is that 85% of the books written out there (by men smarter then me) about business and startups would advise you not to take on a friend as a partner and to also only borrow money from family if you need to. Nevertheless, many small businesses start out their seed money or at least deposit money for a small business loan with funds from family and friends. There is nothing wrong with going down this road, but you need to be cautious.

Always use written communication and actual signed contracts when borrowing any type of money from friends or family. I know I know, its my brother man, everything is cool and we just agreed that when I can pay him back I will once the store opens and we start bringing in money. I sound like my father when I say this but do not let me tell you I told you so. As much as sometimes my parents can drive me insane, when giving advice, as much as I never use to listen in the past, they were almost always right once the full circle came around. It comes from experience and one day you will find yourself in the exact same position talking to your kids and giving them the same advice. Like I have said numerous times already, history repeats and we cannot help ourselves from making the same mistakes that our forefathers made.

Contracts for borrowing money do not have to be 27 pages single-spaced and do not have to involve lawyers and negotiations. It can be as simple as what was mentioned above, just in written form and signed by both the lender and the borrower. I am not saying that your business is going to fail, but it very likely could. The odds are not in your favor unfortunately. There are many successful small business owners out in the world that have no problems and started to succeed from day one. They are they exception however. For every one business that succeeds, ten fail in their place for all controllable reasons. We will talk about that later however, I do not want to get too off topic here in this chapter.

Here is a quick 9 step outline for you to follow to create just a simple agreement between parties:
1- Title your document
2- Name the parties; Borrow (you) and lender (who ever is giving you money)
3- Date the document
4- State the amount of money you are borrowing
5- Describe any interest (if needed)
6- Setup a payment plan & terms. Include the amount of monthly payments, what happens if payments are late, and how long the loan will be for.
7- Describe what will happen if the borrow (you) defaults on the loan (stops making payments).
8- Create a signature block (signature line for both parties to sign)
9- Create a notary block (if needed). Almost all banks have a notary person, which may charge up to $10 for a notary to sign off on the agreement.

There is a basic outline for you to follow for just a basic agreement. I have seen so many families and businesses torn apart because of money issues and I do not wish that kind of stress on anyone. Mainly because their stress could have been completely avoidable if a simple agreement was in place from the beginning before any money changed hands.

I understand it is very easy to say that because you are family it would never get that bad, but please understand that when it does happen, and it most definitely will for most startup small businesses, it can cause many years of family stress not only on yourself, but your entire family. Thanksgiving parties are missed. Christmas parties are not attended. No birthday cards in the mail or phone calls. It can create havoc of what once may have been a great family situation, all because of money.

When I just wrote all because of money in the prior paragraph it made me think of an often-said line; money is the root of all evil. I believe it was my 9th grade English teacher Ms. G., that taught me at the very least to do your own research and got the curiosity part of me to actually look things up on my own and never take things for granted. So I actually looked up that quote to see what its origin was. No surprise when I came to see if was actually a bible quote from Timothy 6:10, but it is actually VERY often misquoted. The actual line is "For the love of money is the root of all evil: which while some coveted after, they have erred from the faith, and pierced themselves through with many sorrows." So next time someone tells you that money is the root of all evil, now you can come back and tell them the true meaning of that saying and where it actually came from. The love of money is the root of all evil.

Ms G. was one of the greatest teachers I ever had in high school and she taught me a lot without really ever teaching me anything if that makes any sense to you. Having a written contract also makes me think of 9th grade as well. I remember this day like it was yesterday and it is still something my friend and I think about. We were in 9th grade English and our teacher was Ms G. We were in the middle of reading Romeo and Juliet in class and the entire class had a HUGE packet of questions to answer. Well it came time to turn our packet in and my friend and I were not quite finished with it. Actually I think I can remember now and say that I was probably not even halfway through the darn thing because I was a lazy freshman and as Ms G. would say, I rested on my laurels. This is where the story gets fuzzy and I cannot prove anything otherwise other then my memories that are quickly fading in my ripe old age of 31. Since we were not finished, we asked if we could have till the end of the day to finish our packet and I thought I remember her saying that we could turn it in by the days end and be ok. Well my friend and I cheated off each other obviously (I believe the statute of limitations on cheating in 9th grade have passed by now) and we finished the packet by the end of school and went to turn it in. Ms G, more then willing to sit down and talk with both of us, just looked at both of us and smiled greatly as she proceeded to scribble 3 lines onto our packets. One vertical line and 2 horizontal lines that seemed to, and from what I could tell from her smile as she chuckled when we pleaded our case about turning it in at the end of the day, turned out to be a bright red letter F. And thus concluded my freshman English class with a D in the class and to never live it down for the rest of my time there in high school.

Freshman year was the worst however I eventually worked my way back up. Senior year I actually took an English class from Ms G as an elective to show her I had changed and I am proud to say that I got an A in that class. So thank you Ms G for helping me figure a few things out in life. So how does this story apply to this chapter? I think it should be pretty obvious that if I had a written contract or agreement stating I had till the end of the day, it would have assisted my friend and I in not receiving an F for a large enough project to bring me down two letter grades at the end of the school year.

Many of us out there may also have family members that do not mind giving you a little money to get your started. Blessed you may be, but if you intend to pay these people back I would still HIGHLY suggest that you even write up a contract stating how much money they are giving you and they are not expecting anything back in return. This can help you out in two different ways. The first, if you become highly successful, do not be surprised if they come asking for money sometime and try to use this situation as a guilt trip to try and get a few extra dollars out of you. The second is that if the business fails, family members can very easily flip-flop on obligations and may expect you to pay back the money they "lost" in your business venture. Once you have that signed agreement or contract, you can just whip it out of that fireproof safe you have guarding all your important paperwork (right? You have one, right? Ok, good.) and then you do not have to be afraid to show up to Thanksgiving and Christmas parties in the future years.

Lesson 5: Choosing a Business Structure

Now we have to decide how you want to setup your business structure. There are a lot of options out there to choose from (four main ones to be specific that I will discuss) and each structure has advantages and disadvantages to them. We will take a closer look at each one and see what those disadvantages and advantages are. It is important to take your time and really learn everything you can about each structure as your business and things you need to do for your business will play hand in hand with the structure you decide to run your business under. As always, there is no right or wrong decision here. You can be sure that many friends and colleagues will have their own opinion about what you should or should not do and everyone is entitled to their opinion. What is important is that you make the best decision on the structure that makes the most sense for you and your business. Now let us dive in headfirst.

Sole Proprietorship

This is by far the most popular structure chosen by most businesses that are not huge corporations. It is also by far the easiest one to setup as far as paperwork and filings are concerned with the state that you live in.

There is no real formal paperwork you usually need to file other than any Licenses and Permits that your business may or may not need. You will need to check with your state business registration to see if any permits of licenses are needed for your specific business. Many people actually could call stuff they do Sole Proprietorship and not even realize it. Do you blog and write constantly as freelance work? Then technically you would qualify as a sole proprietorship. It is not that hard to realize the potential for business. Do you take pictures "professionally" of people and places? Then you could be a sole proprietorship.

As a sole proprietorship you may also do business under a different name then your personal name, which is fine. If you are going to go down that road, all that needs to be done is filing with your state business registration with something known as a trade name or DBA (Doing Business As...). We will touch on this topic a little later, but if you decide to do business under a trade name, make sure you use something unique and check with your state business search online that the name is not actually taken by someone else.

For tax purposes, it stays pretty simple as well. Sole proprietorships are usually either owned by one person or a married couple. 99.9% of the time, with the revenue you generate, its going to go directly through you as your normal "income", so your business is not taxed separately. When you file your yearly taxes, you will most likely just fill out a *Schedule C* form, which is a standard "Profit or Loss from Business" form along with your standard tax forms you do (or should be doing I should say) every year. Now do not think that the "income" you see from your business is not taxable... because it is. Your business is no different than working at a normal job so you still have to pay estimated taxes. Filling out a "self-employment" form as well as a form for "estimated taxes" will complete this task for you. All of these forms can be found on the IRS.gov website if you would like to take a look. Depending on how your business grows, you may find it beneficial to just have someone more familiar with taxes do everything for you. There is nothing wrong with that, just be prepared to pay for it. It usually does not cost much for someone to do your taxes normally (probably anywhere from $50-$200 for your basic taxes). When you start using more forms and talking business taxes, that is where things can get a little more complicated and you can usually save yourself a huge headache if you hire a professional to take a look at everything for you, but like I stated before be prepared to pay for their assistance (in the range of $300-$1,000) just to do your taxes. If you are a Sole Proprietorship that also has employees, you will also need to register with the federal government (IRS) because you will have to pay employer taxes (FICA/Medicare/etc), in which case you will need an EIN number (Employee Identification Number).

So what are the main advantages to Sole Proprietorship? There are a few main topics that I have already touched on. 1) It is easy and fairly inexpensive to setup. 2) You have complete control of your business and what happens to it. 3) Fairly simple tax preparation for most people.

Now what are the disadvantages? 1) The first and probably one that personally scares me the worst is unlimited personal liability. Because as a Sole Proprietor the revenue goes straight to you personally as income, there is no legal separation between you and the business, thus any debts that the business incurs (business loans, credit cards, etc) come directly back onto you if anything bad was to happen. This means that your house, car, and personal assets are on the line for the business, SO BE SMART! The second main disadvantage is that it can be difficult to raise money in the initial stages before you have anything to really show. Many business investors will not usually invest because they will not usually see any real gain that is more than just a general loan. It is not like you can sell stock in your writing ability, right? The correct answer is no, Matt. I cannot sell stock in my sole proprietorship.

The bottom line with Sole Proprietorship is that you and only you are responsible for the success or failure of your business.

Partnership

A Partnership is the next step up from Sole Proprietorship. It is a single business entity that is just owned by two or more people. Keep in mind that if you are a married couple, you can still structure your business as Sole Proprietorship as the government views you as a single entity sharing the stream of revenue/income. Just as each person part of the business shares in the expenses of the business, each partner shares with the gains and losses of the business as well.

When forming a partnership one of the first things you SHOULD do is have some type of legal agreement written up between the both of you. This does not need to involve any lawyers, but you must have a frank discussion with all the owners and decide how decisions will be made, profits and losses split up, adding and deleting (buy out) of current partners, and ultimately dissolving the partnership. This agreement is not mandatory for anything, but I ALWAYS recommend having something agreed upon in writing even if you are working with your best friend(s) or family members.

As a partnership there are normally three different types of partnerships that are created. The first is a general partnership and this is what is legally created if you do not file your paperwork and legal agreements correctly. In a General Partnership all owners share the losses and revenue equally. If there is to be an unequal distribution of this, it needs to be written in the partnership agreement that you complete beforehand.

The second type is a Limited Partnership. This type of partnership basically means that each limited partner has limited liability. With that limited liability however also comes limited decision making decisions and is usually figured out by actual investment dollars of each person. Here is a simple example if you have a limited partnership with three people. Person 1 invests $400, Person 2 invests $500, and Person 3 invests $100... for a total investment of $1,000. Under the Limited

Partnership, Person 1 would own 40% of the business, Person 2 would own 50%, and Person 3 would own 10%. Got it?

The third type of partnership is called a Joint Venture. This is normally only used when a business is going to be open for a specific amount of time, like a 6-month project or 1 year business project. The same basic principles combine here if you understand the basic knowledge of a partnership.

To actually form a partnership takes a little more effort and work then a Sole Proprietorship. You will want to start with looking at your state business register, known as the Secretary of State's Office. There, you will register your business with your name that was agreed upon with your partners. Registering your business is usually pretty inexpensive (in Oregon it costs $100 at the time of this writing). You are more than welcomed to use an outside service to do all this for you, like the website legalzoom.com, but you will pay more than you normally would because above all, they are a business too and what do we all know about the purpose of a business? TO MAKE MONEY! So they will charge you their "fee" to file all this for you. The last time I checked as of this writing to file just a standard business was about $200-$500 depending on what options you chose with them. For many people, having a service do this can be easier and will make sure the necessary paperwork is filled out correctly and is received properly by the state and federal government.

Your yearly obligations in a partnership involve filing an "annual return" that reports your income, gains, and losses. The partnership still does not have to pay income tax as the government still sees the entity as a "pass-through" business, which is similar to a sole proprietorship in that any profits and losses are passed through to the owners/partners. Each partner then must report this on his or her personal taxes. Each partner should receive a *Schedule K* or *form 1065* that shows the basics of profits/loss to the business.

The basic advantages to a partnership are fairly simple and similar to Sole Proprietorship. The first and most simple advantage is that a partnership is still fairly easy and inexpensive to setup in almost any state. One of the most important things to be done is just the partnership agreement. The second advantage is a shared financial commitment (which I guess could also be a disadvantage too depending on how you look at it). Each partner is usually equally invested into the business and equally shares in the profits and losses. Having partners usually means access to more financial stability and also startup capital. The third advantage of a partnership is that a good partnership usually means there is more than one skill set available in the group. Not everyone is a king of all trades. Where one partner may lack, another may thrive. There should be a good balance of skills among the partners to help the business.

There are a few disadvantages to partnership as well though. The first is liability. You and your partners are still liable just like a Sole Proprietorship. You are only liable for your portion or percentage that you own in the business, but that is still something to consider. The second is only applicable if you did not complete a partnership agreement, which is disagreements and dissent among partners. Even the best of friends and family members will get into arguments and simple disagreements about the business. Without a partnership agreement to show who is in charge or who makes decisions, this can cause a large rift among even the closest of friends. So do everyone a favor and ALWAYS have a partnership agreement in place.

Limited Liability Company (LLC)

An LLC is my personal favorite type of business. It takes a little bit more to setup correctly, but the advantages, in my opinion, far outweigh the necessary paperwork in the beginning and yearly filing required. An LLC encompasses the flexibility of a partnership with the limited liability to protect your personal assets. Most states allow even an LLC to be a single owner, so even if you think because you are a single person that you are stuck with a Sole Proprietorship, you would be sorely mistaken. An LLC can consist of either one person, two or more people, corporations or even other LLCs. Just like a partnership, each "owner" receives their portion of the profits and losses, as an LLC is still seen as a "pass-through" business and is not taxed as an entity.

Each individual state may have a few minor differences in requirements but all states follow the same basic principles for starting a business as an LLC. The first thing to you will need to do is choose a name. I might suggest doing the same for a website address that way you can get the same name if you want. There are only three rules when you choose a name for your business as an LLC. The first is that you must include the letters "LLC", this way anyone looking at your business knows you are an LLC. The second is an obvious one that you cannot have the same name as someone else. The third will depend on your state, but most states will not allow certain words in the name.

After a name is selected, you will need to file an Articles of Organization. This document may sound official and difficult, but it really is not. You can find many examples online with just a simple Google search. You can make this form as difficult or simple as you would like. The main portion of this document just includes the name of your business, the official address for the business, and the names of its members. This form is usually just filed with the Secretary of State. Specifically for the State of Oregon, as you go through the online registration process, the state will actually have you go through this basic form online and keeps everything pretty simple.

The next process is not necessarily needed, but is heavily suggested by me if you have more than one person in the LLC. What we are talking about now is called an Operating Agreement. This is very similar to a partnership agreement in that it entails structure of the organization, who is in charge of what, decision making process, percentages of interests between the owners, and other provisions like dissolution, addition of members, or buyout agreements if someone wants to leave. The last thing to do is no different than any other business setup and it includes checking to see if any licenses or permits are needed to start your business.

Taxes work pretty much the same way as a partnership. Because the government does not see an LLC as a separate tax entity, it passes through to its owners and owners pay taxes through their personal tax income tax. Now some states may actually tax the business, most do not, but check your state's income tax agency to be 100% sure. There is a filing requirement each year for your LLC and it depends on how your LLC is setup. If you were a single person LLC, you would file a Form 1040 Schedule C, just like a Sole Proprietor would. If you have more than yourself, then each partner will need to file a Form 1065, just similar to a Partnership business. Always check with a tax professional or the IRS to make sure you file all the necessary paperwork.

There are obviously some advantages and disadvantages to an LLC. The first, and in my opinion, the best advantage is limited liability. This means that the members of the business are protected from personal liability for business decisions or actions taken by the LLC. If you end up incurring debt for the business or are sued for any reason, this protects you and your members from being personally liable. The second advantage is that an LLC can distribute profits as it sees fit. It is up to the members themselves to decide who earns what and what percentage of the profits and losses to distribute.

There are some disadvantages though to an LLC however. The first is a limited life. If you have more than one partner and someone wants to leave, the business is dissolved unless you have a buyout clause in your operating agreement that states otherwise. The second is that you still have to deal with self-employment taxes. So when you take your payment of profits for the end of the year or monthly or whichever you prefer, keep in mind that the money you receive is taxable. Your $50,000 in profit is due to pay some taxes to Uncle Sam. Death and taxes are the only sure thing in life, right?

Corporation

A corporation is an independent legal entity owned by its shareholders. A corporation also is held legally liable for the actions and debts the business incurs. Obviously Corporations are a little more complex with more fees, taxes, and legal requirements. Most of you, if you are reading this, probably do not need to setup a corporation (not yet at least). If you happen to be in that position, then as a corporation, you have the ability to sell ownership shares through offering stock options. Many corporations make the decision to offer an IPO (Initial Public Offering) when they become large enough.

I will not spend a huge amount of time on discussing a corporation as many of you out there that are reading this, are most likely not going to be starting a corporation anytime soon with your business. As like other business structures, you need to file certain documents that will most likely include a little more work than the previous structures.

Some of the advantages of a Corporation are limited liability to protect its shareholders' personal assets against business debts and actions of a corporation. To help raise capital, Corporations can sell stock to raise funds for investment into the company. Corporate taxes are done obviously as the owners of Corporations only pay taxes on corporate profits that are paid to them in the way of salaries, bonuses, and/or dividends. Any other additional profits are taken at a corporate tax rate, which is actually lower than the personal income tax rate.

There are a few disadvantages of a Corporation however. For one, there is double taxation. This happens when a company makes a profit and pays taxes on that profit. Then paying taxes again when dividends are paid to shareholders means double taxation. One other disadvantage that I will mention is the additional paperwork. As corporations are regulated by state and federal agencies, there is usually increased paperwork and recordkeeping that must be done with an entity as opposed to other structures like a Sole Proprietorship, Partnership, or LLC.

Well I believe that wraps it up for structures of a business. I hope this gives you a little more insight into what type of structure you will use on your business. If nothing else, I hope you have learned something new about businesses.

Lesson 6: Writing a Business Plan

Let me start off this chapter by saying there is not just one way to skin a cat, just the same there is no one right or wrong way to write a business plan. I am sure you can find a million different books that tell you how to write a plan and I am not discounting any of them, as there is no truly right answer. There are, of course, a few basic guidelines and things that have to be part of the plan and some things you may or may not want to include at this time. I will try to go over at least the ones that I believe to be the most important. Like I said though, there is more then one way to skin a cat and this is, probably by far, just the basics to give you an understanding of what is yet to come when you sit down to write one of these monsters yourself.

To give you an idea from personal experience, I thought it would be fun to sit down and write out a business plan for my bright idea. This idea was a minor league football league, much like the developmental NBA league is to the NBA. This league would be developmental for football players trying to get into a professional league like the NFL or CFL. I started with the same principals that I will outline in this chapter. After weeks of research and work, I had a finalized product that consisted of about 12 pages of a full business plan as well as 11 pages of a first run promotional packet for teams starting in the league. I spent many months thinking about how I would run a league, how many teams, how many games, the history of failed leagues in the past, and how the league would be structured. It is, in my opinion, a really good starting business plan. I say starting because if I was to take this to an actual investor, I would want to dive a little deeper into my projections and expectations. I can officially say that as I was writing this business plan, there were currently two minor league systems attempting to begin in the United States and one of those leagues was following my business model in preparation for starting their first season in 2014. We will see what league, if any, actually comes to fruition and completes a first season. If you would like to read more about this business plan, you can check out my website at www.brownconsultingwork.com and click on Current Projects.

The other important factor that you must consider is that it is important to spend quality time thinking and writing about your business plan. The business plan not only helps you rationalize your ideas into a product, but also can help you think of so many obstacles and goals along the way you may not have initially thought of. Think back to when you were talking to everyone you knew about this great idea. Most of them probably asked questions that you had not thought about or maybe they asked questions that you could not answer. Either way it does not matter. Their questions are no different then what any other investor or partner is going to ask when looking at your idea and business plan.

One last note before we dive into everything head first. You and a very select few friends and family will probably be the only ones who actually read through your entire business plan. Yes, all of this hard work and research put into a 25-page business plan will most likely go un-noticed. When you look for an initial funding source, like a bank, they will not want to read your 25-page business plan. You can give it to them if you would like and if it makes you feel better, but in the end and almost likely case, it is going to end up in the trash. You will find very few investors that will want to sit down and actually read through your business plan, unless you are paying them, like a consultant, to give you notes and feedback. Almost everyone that you give your business plan to, will most likely just read, if that, your Executive Summary, which is usually a one page summary of your entire idea and plan. Think of this as your cliff notes to your business plan. So now that I have said that, are you ready to begin?

In my opinion, there are seven key areas of your business plan. The first is your Executive Summary. Many books, authors, and business professionals agree that an Executive Summary should be the last thing that you write. Your Executive Summary, like I mentioned above is the cliff notes version of your business plan. Try to keep it to one page in length, but NO MORE then two pages in length. If you go over two pages that it really is not a summary now is it? The Executive Summary can also be seen as the "teaser" to your business plan. Investors and other professionals that read business plans will likely read the Executive Summary and then decide from there whether to read on or throw your business plan to the curb. So you want to make sure you nail and write this as well as possible to engage your reader into keep reading with interest. Lets conquer this section in a little more detail at the end.

The second area of your business plan is the Company Summary. In this section, you will write about who you are and what you are to the company. Most likely you are going to be the sole owner or an executive officer. If you are going to be the sole owner, then in this section, you may want to discuss your qualifications and vision for the company and business. You will want to include some of the basic information about your company; the structure, when it was founded, what state your company will call home, and if you are a business that has already started you could also include some of your recent sales reports and projections in the next few years. If you are going to be an executive officer, you will most likely have partners in this business, so make sure you mention all of them. Talk about each person's experience, why they are a good fit with the company, what they will do for the company. Give a good summary of the nuts and bolts of the business. If you are a brand new company that has not started, you will want to include where you will be located and what kind of facilities you will be getting. Do you need just an office, a workstation at home, or a restaurant location? Give readers a basic overview of what you have in mind and your timeline for starting. If you were to receive funding today, how long would it take you to get into business and start selling? Give a timeline of what needs to happen and how you are going to achieve each objective on that timeline.

The third section is usually where you write about your product or service that you are going to offer. For many businesses, it can be multiple lines of services and products. So you want to list out each product and service with a description. You will often find that if you are looking at getting investors into your business, many investors may not know a single thing about your business, so try to keep things in laymen terms so everyone can understand what you are writing about. As I have discussed earlier in this book back in the idea chapter, you are most likely not the only one person who has had an idea like this or already started a business like yours. How does your business compare to the others? How do your products and services differ from what is already out there. When you cover this topic, do not feel the need to go into too much detail here as your next section will dive deeper into this, but it should at least be discussed in brief if there is direct or indirect competition out there (and there most likely will be). Will you be outsourcing any of your work? How will you fulfill orders that come in? These are questions you may want to conquer in this section. As an apparel store, you will want to discuss where your product comes from, how it is sent over here to sell, and what are your selling techniques. It would be good for EVERYONE if you also picked up a book about selling. If you do not think you need to, then you may just be a little naive. EVERY business is selling something. Even if that "selling something" is getting people to come into your store, you are ALWAYS selling something. Just to get people into an actual store can be a challenge for many businesses. These days, people have too many ways and choices to get things they need. Many people do not even need to leave their house as they can have everything just shipped right to their front door through Amazon, eBay, and pretty much every other website. Most likely you will also be using technology in multiple ways. Whether it is just setting up a website or trying to master social media (don't worry, we will work on this later in the book).

Technology is changing every single day with too many new businesses to keep track of and so many different avenues to go down, it can get very frustrating very fast. How will you cope with all that? Finally, what is the plan for the future? You cannot simply rest on your laurels (Ms G reference) and sell the same product through the years. You will not last longer then two years doing that. Do you have experience in searching out new and different products and technologies to help your business? Do you have any transition plans?

The fourth section (and second most important in my opinion) is the Market Analysis Summary. This is usually the section where many business fail to do any real research about their product and also when many people realize they do not want to move forward after seeing all that is out there for customers to choose from other then their great business idea. You can start off with something simple like identifying your target market. Is your business geared towards kids, teenagers, men 18-35, women ages 50 and up? Simply putting people age 21 and up is not sufficient for you recent college grads out there. Do not waste my time with a stupid sentence like that. It shows me you have put no REAL thought into your business. NOT EVERYONE is going to be a target market. I am not saying that only your target market is going to buy your product or service, but you need to identify who you largest clients are going to be. If you are running a computer repair business, are you going to spend more money advertising at your local video arcade, or would you have more luck advertising in a senior citizen magazine? Think about your target market and who your main customer is going to be. Do your research on market trends. If you are going to open another Mexican restaurant in town, have you noticed there are 4 other Mexican restaurants already open and two that just recently closed because they had not customers. Do not over saturate your market. One of the largest markets that have started out of nowhere are applications for smart phones (iphones and Android). This business did not exist 7 years ago and out of nowhere, there are multiple companies waiting to help you build your own application and advertising companies chomping at the bit to advertise on your application given people and companies a constant stream of income from a simple application that makes a trumpet noise when you blow into the microphone. What does your industry look like? Are you opening a fast food business? If so, take a look at the market analysis of fast food. Are you bringing something new to your area or are there already enough McDonalds locations at each corner? One of the most important questions in this section is going to be where you discuss your main competition. Who is going to be directly competing with you and how are you going to win the competition? No, burning the competition's business to the ground is not an appropriate answer to this question. In 100% of any business, there is competition and most likely direct competition right across town. How is your business going to succeed in getting customers over to your store instead of the other? Who are your competitors and what do they have that you do not. Why are people going to them and not you? This leads us into the next section of your business plan.

The fifth section of a business plan is your Strategy Summary. First start out continuing to discuss your competition. Review what your target market is and why you believe it is the best target market for your product. An important strategy to discuss in this section is to answer how you will get people to come back for repeat service and products. Be as specific as your can, if not for your reader, for yourself. Like I mentioned before, this business plan in its entirety may only be read by a few people, so this is your brainstorming session about how you want to run your business. How will you develop that loyalty to your product and business? What is your plan to keep track of these strategies, or can you? The answer better be yes to that last question, otherwise you have some more explaining to do. If you cannot track your loyalty or strategies for your business to succeed, then you may need to take some more business classes. If you are on top of everything, you have probably already thought about tracking purchases and being able to see by customer who has purchased what. This may help you analyze what customers are buying the most and more importantly, what customers are NOT buying so you can replace or change that product and/or service to become more profitable.

The sixth section of your business plan should be a Management Summary. If you are going to setup a sole-ownership business, this may be one of your shortest sections, as it does not take much to explain that you are going to be the sole owner and operator for the business. You possibly may not even need this section if you are a sole ownership business because you already addressed this back in section two, Company Summary. If you are a business with multiple owners however, you will need to discuss a few key topics like the structure of your organization. Who is going to be in charge of who and what? Who is going to be your management team and executive management team, because there is definitely a different between the two. What is your personal plan? Are you going to be the CEO leading the charge, or would you be a finance guy like myself, possibly a CFO. Make sure when you address these team members that you give a little bit of their history and why you believe they will be successful in their position with your company.

The seventh and final section (and I believe the MOST important) is your Financial Plan. This is where many people may need assistance from an actual consultant like myself to at least review their plans and make sure they have thought of everything possible. It is never a good thing when you build your business on a model you created, then come to find out in a review process by someone else, possibly an investor, there is an error in your formula and your break-even analysis is actually much worse. At the VERY LEAST in this section you should include a Break-Even Analysis of your business. In a nutshell, your revenue minus expenses equals your net. Do not forget to pay yourself in this equation too. This is where you will address how you intend to get your initial seed money for financing this project. You can always include more then the bare necessities and I recommend that. If nothing else, it helps people see that you have really done your homework on your finances, which can be the main determinant on an investor looking at your business. An investor's first question will always be how do I make my money back? If you are looking for investors, obviously make sure you include that with your financial information. Be sure to look into the future of at least five years. It may be difficult to identify where things may be in the first five years, but it is important to at least show a long-term plan of where you believe you will be in five years.

After all is said and done, you can now go back and write your Executive Summary. It should include a basic overview of your business, your business plan, strategies, and financial plan. It is a good idea as well to include your overall business objective and possibly some things to show how you will succeed in completing that objective.

After that, I believe you should be done. I will mention this again like I did when we began this chapter; there is no right or wrong way to write a business plan. What I have written here is just a basic outline of what I believe is the best way to complete a true business plan. There are many other authors and people with more experience and more education then myself that have written books specifically about writing a business plan. I encourage you to at least look at a few just to get some ideas of where to start.

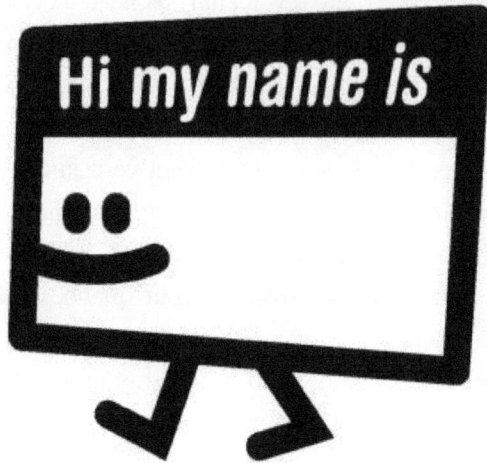

Lesson 7: Secure Your Name and Logo

Does your business name matter? YES! There is a lot that can be said about a name in business or personal life. For example, think of someone you hate… well hate is a strong word, how about someone you just dislike. Got their name in your head? Ask yourself, every time you hear that name, do you think of that person? The answer is usually yes. So there is your evidence that a name matters. How do people or companies come up with their names? Well that can take the form of many different answers to be honest with you. There can be a lot to say about your business name. You can even buy a specific book just to help you come up with a great business name if you want to spend the money. Well I guess you did spend money to buy this book, right? Or are you reading a free copy? Its ok either way… even if I gave you a copy as a gift, it's a tax write-off for me… so I still come out ahead in some respect. More on that later when we talk about finances though.

You can probably spend an entire year reading books from different experts who all end up saying different things. Some people may believe that the best route to go is some type of abstract name that you can then build into an image that is your company. For example, let us take the name "Sage". This is an idea of an abstract word for a company that could mean almost anything in the world; it just depends on how you spin it with a good marketing strategy to your customers. Other experts may say that your business name should tell your customer exactly what your business is. For example let us use "Sage Financial Software." Well it's pretty obvious that your company makes financial software isn't. Think right now about a few names of companies both that could be construed as abstract and informative, as there are way to many out there to name in a single book, or at least a book that anyone would read or possibly purchase. The fact still remains that whatever name you decide to use can be successful; it strictly depends on how it is marketed to the public that will make or break your business name. Even a horrible name marketed the correct way can end up being successful.

If you have the money to spare, you can always hire a company to figure out a name for you, but be prepared to pay a pretty penny. Usually a service like this could cost you anywhere from $60,000+. With a service like this, you are usually getting a little more then just a name of your business. Hiring a company to do this would give you access to such things as trademark laws and other legal words and big phrases that even I do not understand sometimes. It also usually includes a logo design or a few possible ideas for you to use. Be careful however about companies that do not charge much. As with life, you usually get what you pay for and a cheaper company that sells its services for $50 may not have access to researching naming rights, which could potentially cost you money in the future if there is another already established company out in the world.

In my personally partially educated and somewhat started career, I find it easier to have a business name and catchphrase that tells my customer what my business is. The reason for this is because it means less time for me having to explain what my business does when people ask about it. Think long term as well for your name. If you were to name your startup, Portland Oregon Software Company, that is great. Then what happens if your company becomes too large and has to relocate to Seattle? Then the name Portland Oregon Software Company would just be meaningless, right? Two more tidbits of a suggestion for you, 1) do not use words in your name that are abstract or involve puns that only you know or is an inside joke between you and your wife, and 2) Do not use things like LLC or Inc if your business is not really this type of business. Do not use LLC if your company is not a limited liability company; do not use Inc if your business is not really incorporated. These are just a few simple suggestions, but some that many people can make when brainstorming ideas of a business name.

Here are a few examples of some popular business names and how they got their names:

NIKE: is named for the Greek goddess of victory and the swoosh symbolizes her flight.

SKYPE: the original name was actually "sky-peer-to-peer", which then was shortened into "Skyper", and then it eventually became "Skype"

ADIDAS: was taken from the founder Adolf Dassler, who's first name was shortened to get ADI, then the first three letters of his last name DAS, hence ADIDAS

7-ELEVEN: was originally named "U-TOTE'M" up until 1946 when the hours of the stores extended from 7:00 AM until 11:00 PM

AMAZON: Founder Jeff Bezos wanted his company name to start with the letter A, this way it would come up first alphabetically. He searched through the dictionary until he came to the word Amazon. He thought the Amazon was the biggest river in the world and that is what he dreamed is company would be

INTEL: simply shorted from Integrated Electronics

COCA-COLA: Derived from its flavoring of Coca Leaves and Kola nuts. The original founder changed the K in Kola to C to make it look more appealing

SONY: from the Latin word "sonus" that means sound

STARBUCKS: named after a character in Moby-Dick

VOLKSWAGEN: means people's car in German

WENDY'S: the nickname of founder Dave Thomas' daughter Melinda.

Hopefully those ideas were enough to get your blood pumping a little and come up with some ideas about your own business. One final suggestion would be that once you have a list of four or five names, do not be afraid to get feedback from family members, friends, and the general public. That may be the best way to decide on a final name for your company. Do not be afraid to go with your gut thought if something really resonates with you.

Lesson 8: Looking for Money

Now that you have figured out what kind of business you are going to have (LLC I assume?) and you have written a business plan with every aspect of the business discussed in length, now it is time to start looking at finances. Let us also assume by this time you have followed my previous chapter about getting yourself cleaned up both credit wise and also personally. I am going to talk about a few different ways you can look for money for a startup company. Depending on your actual business you may or may not want to use one of these options for a variety of reasons or its possible your actual business may not be eligible to receive some types of finances. So let the rocks fall where they may and we will just get started on this endless journey, because… you are not even halfway through my book.

One of the most obvious places that people start is with their local small business association (www.sba.gov). This is a great website for anyone new or old starting their business. You will find a ton of information about starting a business as well as links to plenty of legitimate places to look for financing. I promise you that you could spend an entire week searching on the Internet for a legitimate business loan for startups. If you are even thinking of getting financed and are looking for a loan with no money down you might as well close this book now and use it as a fire starter. It still amazes me that people talk about starting a business with no money down or people that obviously are the "dreamers" that will spend their entire life dreaming and talking but never actually doing anything about it or have the means to do anything about it.

One way is plastic. Yes, credit cards. It can sometimes be your only friend if you want to do everything on your own and not take out a loan or are not able to get a loan in any traditional way. Many businesses (including Google) were started on credit cards. For the first year and a half, the owners financed Google through credit cards. Now obviously that business turned out well. It should not surprise you though that for every startup business that fails there are at least eight to ten businesses that fail. When you fail, you usually fail pretty big too, which means paying back that money for many years (if you can) or worst case declaring bankruptcy. So I urge you to tread very carefully if you are intending on using your plastic swords of money to finance a business startup. As a reminder, even though you may have your company setup as an LLC to protect your personal liability, if you use your personal funds (like a credit card with your personal name on it, your waive your liability for that expense). If you have a credit card that is specifically with your business, you may still be in luck. Keep that in mind if you are using plastic.

One of the first places people look is usually family and friends. This can be difficult for some people depending on you personally and your specific situation. Obviously every person has a different type of family so telling you how I have dealt with family situations would not necessarily work for you. If you have a trusting family and group of friends that truly believe in your business and its success they will probably be likely to give you at least a little start towards your goal amount you need to get started on your business. As I mentioned back in a prior chapter though, be careful about the terms of your loan and

ALWAYS have a written contract, even if it is your brother or best friend. Money has a tendency to really cause rifts and arguments between friends and especially family. Lets not make Thanksgiving too much bitter then it could already be with personalities.

Bank loans are a more traditional source for startup businesses, but be prepared to put at least some sort of significant down payment towards the loan for your business. Banks are usually a long shot unfortunately because many people do not have enough to cover a down payment amount the bank is asking for. Another restriction you may run into is that even though your bank may tout the "#1 small business lender", they leave out the little details that say your business must be active for two years and/or show a certain amount of revenue quarterly or annually. You can however, check with your local SBA for a SBA Guaranteed Loan, meaning your loan may be able to get some assistance from the SBA. Even with that though, do not be surprised if your local or national bank still denies you the loan. My reminder earlier about credit cards and an LLC applies to bank loans as well. To keep your liability your loan needs to have your business's name, not your personal name, otherwise you waive your liability. This is another snafu you may run into with a bank, because they may want a personal guarantee from you to get the loan. Anytime your personally guarantee something with your business (even an LLC) you waive your liability.

Grants may be another route to look for if you have a specialized business, like something in technology. There are some federally funded programs that have money specifically set aside for technology research grants and that forces some high-tech companies to specifically set aside money in their budgets to help high-tech companies with inventions that a company may want to actually use in the future.

Angel Investors are another great source, if you can actually get a hold of one. I have done a little research on Angel Investors and there are definitely people out there with money to waste and looking for things to invest in. Angel Investors will usually ask for a high percentage back when repayment begins, but they have the right to because you are borrowing their personal money and they are actually willing to take the personal on you. Please remember my comment earlier with a personal guarantee because that also stands in this instance as well. If you personally guarantee the loan with an angel investor, you are personally liable for that loan. Needless to say be careful with your choice of words and answering questions in the right manner. Using Google, or any other search engine by that mind, you can easily search for "Angel Investors" and come up with millions of options. Many links will have a main website where you must pay $100-$300 to post your business idea up for angel investors to look at. This is not uncommon. Other sites may have you send your business plan and be one of three selected to do a short presentation to a panel of angel investors. This is common as well. Be careful and make sure to do your research on the website you are using though, as there are many scammers out there and many people that are just waiting online to take your money. Use the old basic rule that if it sounds too good to be true, then it usually is.

Kickstarter and other similar websites have become very popular nowadays. If you are not familiar with these sites, check them out. They are very worthwhile! In a nutshell, it is a website where you can create a quick website page about your business (even uploading a video if need be) and put it out into the world looking for people to invest. You set your own goals to raise funds and you have the option of adding gifts to those who invest, like the first product off the assembly line, etc... or pre-purchasing your consumer goods as well. I am reminded of a local shoe company in my area that has started a few different Kickstarter campaigns that were very successful. They have started selling their initial inventory as part of their investment. If you decide to go this route (which I will always suggest at least doing something like this on the side), remember that if you sell merchandise as part of the investment, make sure you are set to deliver!!! Do not start off your business by screwing over customers that initially invest in your business online. Reward them for being the first ones in.

One last option may be de-cluttering your house of useless objects that you bought in your twenties or college items you are still holding on for sentimental reasons (god only knows why). Now my wife will be the first to tell you that I throw too much stuff away and many times I have gotten in trouble for throwing away something we or she needed. Oops, sorry honey! Use sites like Craigslist to sell all that useless crap and use that money as your investment or down payment. Do you really use that treadmill anymore? Have you heard of running outside? Are you holding onto a few old laptops possibly? Even things like old baseball cards that you have not looked at for twenty plus years may be worth something to someone. To some extent, everything has a price and it's just a matter of finding that one person that is interested in something you have.

This should at least get you started in thinking about how you are going to finance your business now. Do not be afraid to ask for help, especially to other small businesses you know of. Not everyone is successful in a month or even 6 months to one year. It is important to remember to just stay on track and be true to your business. If it is truly a good idea, the money will come.

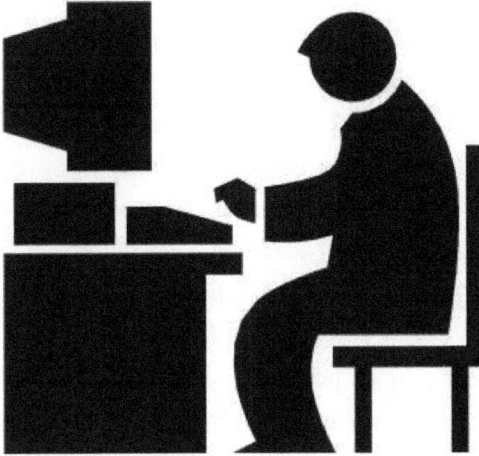

Lesson 9: Creating a Website

Creating a website for your business can seem like a daunting task for many people out there especially if you are not that tech savvy. In today's technological world though you do not have to be a genius to have a great website for your business. It really just depends on how in depth you want your website. Are you looking for an e-commerce type site where customers can purchase things directly from your website? If so, that is fine and it is still possible for you to offer this with your own knowledge and research. The more in depth you think you want to go or if there is something specific you want on your website that you do not know how to do, do not hesitate to call a professional.

Many people you probably already know either can create a decent website or know someone in the business that can create one for you. If this is your first attempt at making a website, you may feel like you are in over your head. For beginners I always like to suggest wordpress.com where you can create a website and/or blog for your business. If you do not know what a blog is, its just a fancy word for an online journal. You can write posts and as many as you would like, similar to news stories. I use wordpress for my own business site and once I took the time to really just play around with the different buttons and options, it ended up being very easy. Wordpress can help set you up with your domain and everything else in between. For a dedicated web address to your business, something with a .com or .net or .org, you should expect to pay around $18 per year on wordpress, which is pretty good considering everything they offer. If you are really in a pinch you can get a free web address that contains yourbusinessname.wordpress.com. Do yourself a favor and just spring for the extra $18 a year charge.

I'm going to give you at least a few points to keep in mind as you brainstorm what your website may look like when you come to this point. I should have probably started off by asking if your business is going to have a website. Are you? The answer most definitely should be yes, otherwise you are setting yourself up for failure. Having a website can give you access to an entire different demographic of customers you may not have even seen on your best day. Creating a website for your business can be free publicity and free advertising, especially if you do things right in social media sites like Facebook, Twitter, Pinterest, and many more. We will cross that road of using social media in an upcoming chapter. I felt, in this day, to leave social media in its entirely separate category since it has now become a huge platform within themselves with each of them offering something different to you and your business.

BRAINSTORM. Lets start by keeping this simple. First you need to brainstorm what you want your site to look like. Are there websites out there currently that you like the look of? Go to a few of them and actually think about why you like them so much. Is it the layout of the page, ease of use and navigation, maybe the colors seem soothing to you instead of bright colors on a bright pallet. I suggest when you are brainstorming ideas that you use a blank piece of paper and at least draw the layout of your page. Where will your main navigation buttons be? Most people put their navigation bars at the top of the page, however others prefer that the navigation be on the side of the page. There is no right or wrong answer really, it is just a matter of opinion and trial and error to see what your customers may like best. Whatever type of navigation bar you come to the conclusion of, just make sure it is easy to navigate. Customers, and me personally, cannot stand when it takes us more then TWO clicks to get exactly what we are looking for. Did you read that correctly? Yes, I said TWO clicks to get to where any customer may need to be. In the very worse circumstance, and depending on the complexity of your business, I would be satisfied with three clicks, but if you are thinking of having more then that, you might as well not waste your time in your current thought and layout and start all over, because you have failed faster then an armless man trying to play tennis. Sorry if that sounds rude, but lets face it, the armless man tends to not even attempt to walk onto the court... where you already have by starting your layout thought a brainstorming process and drawing.

CONTACT. Always make sure that your website has a contact me button or page so that customers can get in touch with you. It is amazing to me the number of businesses out there with websites that do not or forget to put their contact information on the site. I am not sure if they just forgot or are assuming that because I found their website that I know how or where to contact them. We all know what happens when we assume, so never assume and make sure people know where to go to get in touch with you. Adding an address to your business, phone number if applicable, and email are the bare minimum you should make available to your customers if you are a truly legitimate business.

Many people may ask if they need a website depending on your business. Say you own a food cart in town or a locally owned convenient store. Do you really need a website even if no one is going to "buy" anything online from you? YES! Even if your website is a single page with a concise message and logo of your food cart with a menu and location, that is just fine. As long as your have something to show online and to share on social media, that is what you are looking for. There is

NOTHING wrong with just having a single page website if that is what your business calls for.

QUALITY. One of the most important aspects is about QUALITY CONTENT and NOT QUANTITY. Do not fill your page with pop-up ads, banner ads, and other meaningless content that does not have anything to do with your business. It will really cause customers to leave your site and in some cases, not want to shop at your store. Yes, people can be that pity that if you have a poor enough website, they have no interest in ever going into your store. I can be one of those people at times. Guilty as charged.

SEO. Search Engine Optimization. Do not use pictures as links to your subpages. Search engines will not understand your pictures when people search for something in your business. Use text links that say exactly what they are clicking into. A simple word "Pictures" can link to a page with pictures of your products and/or services. Make sure you fill out the "tags" section when creating a post as this helps search engines find relevant posts in your website. SEO can also pertain to your website tags when someone uses a search engine. Talking about SEO could probably be a chapter all in itself, but it mainly is about using words to describe what is on your site to help search engines find it easier. There are several professionals that can help you achieve a better SEO, but be prepared to probably pay at least a finger if not a full arm and leg for their help.

BRANDING. Do not forget to "brand" your website with your logo and business colors if those are applicable. Making your logo prominent on every page can create a memory stick in a customer's mind. Make the logo prominent on every page but at least have some sort of smaller logo on the sub-pages (sub-pages mean every page other then the homepage).

LINKS. If your website is going to have external links (links to other websites other then your own), make sure that these links open up in new windows. As much as sometimes I hate this, I know why websites do this. If you do not know, its so you have to come back to their website to close your browser. It ensures a gentle return from you as a customer. Making sure the website stays in front of the customer is a key aspect to that memory stick you are looking to build with your business along with everything else in your website.

SEARCH. For many business this may not apply, but if your website ends up becoming somewhat of a monster for even you, you should consider the application of a "search" button within your website. I know wordpress offers this option to you automatically with your blog and it is something you can turn off and on at your own demise either way. If you end up having a complicated website, a search feature will come in handy for your customers and is a convenient way for customers to type in exactly what they are looking for.

ABOUT. Surprisingly one of the most popular pages on any site is the "About" page. Simply put, this is because people are curious as a cat. I guess that is why they call you whiskers, right? If your business is about you personally, like a consulting website, include information like your background and how it pertains to your business and makes you successful. If you are an actual business, include things like when your store opened and why you opened the store. This is where you can tell people when and where you thought of that great idea. It is a great page to share that story and whatever else you want to. The about page can help ease a new customer with warm fuzzy feelings inside as they learn more about you and your business. Making them feel warmer about your business or yourself will make them have an easy decision process about using your business.

SIGN-UP. This is another option that wordpress can offer to your fans. By entering an address then can automatically be notified when a change happens to the website or a new post is put up on your page. Make sure your website has SOMETHING like this because it is essentially free advertising for your business and advertising directly to a customer that has an interest in you and your business.

OPTIMIZE SIZE. I know those HD pictures are great and yes, they look fantastic blown up to an uncommon huge size too big to fit through a door. PLEASE for my own sanity, check the size and download times on your website. NOTHING is worse then waiting for a website to load. In these days, people are used to getting their information at the snap of a finger. The fact that we have to wait 10-15 seconds for your website to load is absurd. Slow uploading websites are usually caused by graphics that take too much time to load or large sized pictures on your website. For example, do you have a specific homepage on your browser? I know I do. My homepage is Google and it is not because I like to search for stuff. It is because it is the fastest loading website. There are no fancy graphics or pictures, just a plain white background, the words Google, and a search input. It's beautiful every time I open up my browser. It's beautiful because it loads up in less then a second. Keep this in mind on your website. I am not saying that you cannot have pictures or graphics, just be careful in what you choose and the size of them as well.

STATS. Wordpress usually offers this at no extra cost to you. You can track how many clicks you get every day, even narrowing it down by each day and what pages specifically have been hit. Find out what day of the week is your most popular day. My guess would be Monday morning because people are just coming to work and do not feel like working, so they waste time on the Internet. The other most popular time may be Friday afternoon, for the obvious reason that people are done working for the week and just want the business day to be over, so they waste time searching on the Internet. Just for kicks and your own knowledge, understand also that TUESDAY is statistically the most productive day of the week.

Well I believe that covers some of the basic tips on building a great website for your business. I know I laid out a lot of tips and guidelines, but these are just my personal thoughts and if you want to do something different, you have every right to. Be creative and have fun. I look forward to look at what you come up with Monday morning or Friday afternoon!

Lesson 10: Social Media

For many young guns out there, Social Media is something we now live with everyday, constantly checking out Facebook posts, twitter feeds, and instagram following friends and celebrities in their everyday lives, which can be both good and bad for anyone out there. Businesses have started trending now and following suit with their own Facebook pages and twitter accounts as they try to stay relevant in today's culture by trying to connect to a younger consumer. Many brands and companies now have entire departments and staff specifically for social media. It is a growing job in any industry and one that does not seem to be going away anytime soon.

For many older generations though, the Internet can seem like a vast amount of information out in wonderland and you have no idea of even the difference between MySpace and flickr, let alone still living in the world of Hotmail and GeoCities back in the mid 1990s'. We need to keep in mind that although it may seem to many of us that social media has been around for your entire life, for others, it is still something new to learn. So let us start with a brief history of social media and the

Internet and then we can go into a little more detail on some of the more important applications for your business to focus on at first.

It's hard to believe that the World Wide Web only went public back in 1991, when I was just eight years old. Even at that time many people never used it, as it required skills that many people did not have at the time. The first major user-used website was email and was introduced as Microsoft Hotmail back in 1997. I remember the frenzy, as it was my freshman year of high school. AOL was quick to follow later in 1997 and really brought instant messaging to the forefront of computer users and communication. In 1998, one of the now largest companies started up, known as Google. It was a huge moment to say the least and remember it was financed through credits cards of the two main owners at the time of its start. I think that investment has more then paid off now, wouldn't you say? Shortly after in 1999, Naptser hit the scene and created an uproar among many individuals and music creators/fans. For those who do not know about Naptser, it was a file sharing program where anyone in the world could share music and you would never have to buy a CD again. Obviously many record companies and artists fought against it and eventually won, but not before the music world was changed for better and worse. Websites like photobucket and LinkedIn started in 2003, but never really caught on with the masses like MySpace did in 2003 when it began. Starting in 2003 we started now seeing many companies popup over the next several years that are some of the largest social media sites to date, including Facebook in 2004, YouTube in 2005, Pinterest in 2010, Twitter in 2011... thus building the Internet population to over 2.4 Billion users that span across the globe connecting with a single click of a mouse.

I am sure if you stepped into your local bookstore, you could find books among books about social media and specifically books probably about each application and website on its own as there is a real ton of information out there on what people believe is the correct and wrong ways to use social media platforms in your business. If you have the time and money, feel free to buy each one and read it cover to cover. I definitely do not have the money nor the luxury of time to read a ton of books and a specific book on each platform to learn the ins and outs of everything. Feel free to forge ahead and go buy some of those books now. You can pick up here where you left off next year or some years later when you finish reading all those other books. Otherwise, you can keep reading and at least get a birds eye view of two of the main platforms being used today, which is Facebook and Twitter.

FACEBOOK

There is no easy or exact answer to the question you may ask, does my business need Facebook. Yes, the answer is obviously YES, but it needs to be used correctly. There are definitely some things to consider when you start a Facebook page for your business.

First off, you can create a Facebook "page" in which you can make posts by writing, posting pictures, and even setting up events. The fans of your page are the actual Facebook users out in the world. Its up to you to find those "likes" though for your page, which can take a lot of consuming time out of your day. Having a Facebook page just to be on Facebook is useless. It will not do you any good, if you are never on it, never make posts, or stay altogether quiet on the western front of Facebook social media. Facebook can be a great marketing tool if used correctly and effectively. It can be fairly inexpensive and somewhat free depending on how your marketing ideas are about getting customers and fans to your business page.

Do not think of a "fan" as a "customer". That is a mistake that MANY businesses make when they setup a page on Facebook. When a user clicks "like" on your page, they may not necessarily be a direct customer of yours. One of the great things about Facebook and their marketing tools is that you can identify specifically what market group you want to target. If you are looking specifically for females 20-29 years of old, you can specifically setup a marketing plan through ads on Facebook that will automatically go directly to that marketing group. Now whether they click on your "like" button can depend on many things.

I won't bore you with the step-by-step directions on how to create a page on Facebook as I am pretty sure you are tech savvy enough to follow their directions and create a Facebook page in as little as a few minutes. One suggestion I would give you when you create a Facebook page for your business, is always think about interaction with your customers/fans. When creating things like a Discussion board, uploading images, videos, you should be constantly thinking about how you are going to interact with your fans. Do not just post a picture by itself, put a small description and ask for comments by saying something as simple as "what do you think?" Asking open ended questions will help create an interaction between you and your fans that could possibly turn into customers after their interaction with your facebook page.

Many businesses find success in creating a platform for customers to create content, like drawings, pictures, and videos. Having customers and fans create content that you post on the page and your website helps create interaction as these fans believe them as being involved with your business, creating a self sense of vindication and loyalty towards your brand and business. Do not be afraid to use such measures when you are getting started asking for votes on a few different profile pictures or small contests and other things like that.

Many business owners already have personal accounts on Facebook, which you can link to your business page. Make sure that you encourage all of your friends to like your business page by inviting everyone. You can even encourage them to share the page on their wall and postings to get more fans. Make sure you have integrated your Facebook page onto your website as well. This can be done very easily though wordpress as well as any other website creating application. Like we discussed earlier, Social Media has become a way of doing business for many businesses out there, so standards like Facebook "like" buttons and sharing buttons are a common thing on websites now so people can share pictures and posts that you make on your website.

No mater what fad comes out every couple years about marketing, the truly best way to gain popularity, more fans, and more customers is word of mouth marketing. It is a tried and true method when done correctly. We all have friends out there that are always telling us about this great new restaurant that just opened, or this new drink they tried at the local supermarket. Link your Facebook page to any business email and include the link on any newsletters and articles as well.

The most important thing to remember with using Facebook as your business is to always be engaging with your fans. Many small ideas that might help in the beginning is a weekly contest for something like a small giveaway they pickup at your place of business. Doing polls about certain products or preferences of your customers. With social media, you are given direct access to potential customers and for many businesses social media is a great way to get customer reactions to new products and help introduce the latest and greatest thing from your business.

TWITTER

Twitter is probably the second most important social media application your business should be using to help market your business. For those who do not know what Twitter is, in a nutshell, it is place to post short blogs (called Tweets) out into the world of twitter. Your post is limited to 140 characters (letters/symbols) and is posted to your main page that is then followed by others out in the twitter universe. Although Twitter does share some common tools with Facebook, Twitter can be used in its own unique way for any business.

A few simple suggestions for you when you start your twitter account: 1) Make sure the look and feel of your twitter account resembles your Facebook and website. Have all three in a similar scheme (colors/logos/etc). This will help brand your business and make you more noticeable when users come across your marketing and being able to easily identify your business from its look and feel.

There are two main photos to consider when setting up your twitter account. The first is your profile picture, which many businesses do different things. Simply using your company logo is acceptable, but some businesses choose to add a personal photo of the founder/CEO/etc to put a personal touch onto the business. What you do with your account is you choice. The second picture is the profile header, which is the large background image that will be used when people view your twitter page. This is essentially just a background image and might I suggest a similar image to whatever you used on your actual website, this way it creates a tie-in with your website, building that familiarity aspect between the two.

Make sure that when you create your profile you take the time to fill out ALL the information. You want to make sure and put the most necessary information like contact info, Facebook page, website, etc on your profile so twitter followers can know where to go to get more information on you and your business. One of the easiest ways to start getting followers is to follow people yourself through your twitter account. Many twitter folks will follow each other as an unwritten rule to help build your audience. As a general rule when you start following people, stick with customers you may know of, business partners, suppliers, contractors, your competitors, and other businesses in your neighborhood.

As you get started with twitter, it can be a somewhat daunting task for some until they get used to the twitter universe. As a general rule you want to try and find your sweet spot between the different types of tweets you send out into the world. The most basic is a general tweet out to everyone that follows you. If you receive messages (or mentions) on your twitter account, make sure to respond back even with just a simple thank you. Interaction is the key to twitter. If you never interact with people, you cannot expect then to interact initially with you. Always try and drive traffic to your website, Facebook, and other platforms. And on a side note, you should be doing the same on your other platforms as well. Always be cross promoting your business to anywhere that will listen.

Social media is all about building brand loyalty to your business. You are trying to connect with your customers and fans to create a lasting impression and one that you hope will make them think about your business when they need something you might sell. It is a constant job on top of everything else you may be doing with your new business.

Many small businesses may find it useful to hire (if you have the money available) a professional firm to manage the social media aspect of your business. Do not expect them to do this for free however, as most companies charge a monthly fee for ongoing maintenance and building of your brand or business and the prices may surprise you in a bad way. I recently talked with a local business that does just this sort of thing for many small businesses and their rates started at $500 per month, per customer. So do not be surprised if you find businesses that will charge the same if not more for what they offer to do. Just remember that if you decide to go this route, shop around and see what everyone has to offer. You do not have to stay local either. The beauty of technology is that anyone, anywhere can access a twitter and Facebook page to do work. All it takes is an Internet connection.

Lesson 11: Marketing

I have debated for quite some time how to properly right a chapter on marketing. I am obviously not the first cat out of the bag to write about marketing and I will be the first to admit there is more people out there better versed at this then me. However, I believe it is worth at least trying to talk about it in this book, as it is an essential part of business. So what I have decided to do is jump around a little to give you all some general ideas on marketing and what your business could be doing for little to no cost and then a few ideas that would obviously cost more money. A marketing plan always starts out with having a dollar amount in mind that you and your business are willing to spend. You are never going to get everything you want, especially for the price that you want to pay. That is just a fact of life. So let us jump into the deep end and get started.

You will always be better if you offer something different in your product. Do not just come out and give everyone the old "me too" phrase and try to jump into line. If you have the same product and price of your competitors without anything to differentiate your products, you are just fooling yourself into becoming successful with your business.

The size of your business and/or company is a good and bad thing no matter how big or small you are. We have all seen the usual marketing ploys by firms both large and small. Small firms tend to exploit the flaw of personality and personal attention to larger firms. Large firms exploit the broad experience and faster response times compared to smaller firms. There are positives and negatives to being both. The situation that your specific business has to answer to consumers is that no matter what your size is, why does it matter to me?

You do not always have to hire the people with the best ideas, just the ideas themselves and make them successful. Trying to hire all the latest big shot idea makers could make you go insane and broke at the same time. Instead, if you see a business idea out there that you believe you can make successful, buy the idea and not the man behind it. Don Kingsborough, the man behind the success of Teddy Ruxpin and Lazer Tag said it best, "You cannot hire enough people so that you have all the good ideas. That is a bad concept. I think the right concept is to figure out who has the best ideas and figure out what you do best. You concentrate on that, and if someone else has a good idea, buy it and make it successful."

Stick heavy on local marketing ideas. Google is a great place to start as they have actually begun in the last couple years to really make more of an emphasis on local content when searching for products and services. This could be as simple as claiming your FREE business listing on sites like Google Places and FourSquare. For those that are unaware of FourSquare and because I have not discussed this at all in my book yet, it is basically a search location website for businesses and people, using a "search nearby" field that you would type in Burgers and it would locate places you could get burgers within a certain distance of where you are at. Google Places is basically the same thing. But if nothing else, this is FREE for you to register your business. One option for businesses is to join your local chamber of commerce. Although not free usually (around $300 a year depending on your city), this can be a good resource for you meeting people and other businesses in the local area. There are often events held throughout the year you can attend and often your chamber of commerce will offer classes in a variety of different business subjects throughout the year that are usually offered for free or a low registration cost. Yelp is another website that is free for businesses to sign up. Users can put reviews and rate your business along with location services when searching for products and services.

SEO is probably a term some are familiar with, but if you do not know what I am talking about, SEO stands for Search Engine Optimization. These are basically keywords on your website that help search engines find you. This may be something you actually hire out to do unless you are well versed in website building and familiar with SEO. This can usually cost anywhere from doing a simple trade of services for someone to upwards of $500 depending on where you look. If you are going to hire someone to help you with this, be sure about their qualifications and ask for references because it is very easy to find someone on craigslist that will promise you the world and ends up messing things up further then what you already had setup.

Constant updates can drive you and consumers up a wall. Personally if I am following a business I expect to see at least some hits of advertising a few times a week on sites like Facebook and Twitter, which will be your main sources of free web advertising. This can be done a variety of ways from just simple blogging about your business to daily updates on specials. What I see as most popular is bloggers from small businesses that will start a daily or weekly blog about them or their business. If you begin blogging, you will get frustrated with the lack of interest in the beginning from customers and will eventually meet the point of no return when you decide to stop blogging because you do not see any real results from it. This is the demise of many bloggers. The key is to stay persistent and keep going even when no one is reading your blog. Blogging may not sound as sexy of a marketing plan but it is also free and blogs do not need to be any certain amount of length, possibly even just a paragraph long about your business. If that is your case, what is the hurt in keeping it going as I doubt it takes that long for you to write up a paragraph on something about your business and post it to Facebook and Twitter. Remember that a large majority of web traffic still begins from general searches, so your blog is bound to come up if you are utilizing your SEO tools properly.

If you are a penny pincher, you will probably stick to easy and free opportunities like Facebook, Twitter, Instagram, FourSquare, and several other social media sites yet to come up tomorrow. When you use social media, remember that the key to become successful is in its title; social. Build relationships with customers; create conversations with your customers and colleagues. Be engaging with your social media tasks. Customers want to purchase products and services from business and people that they trust and like.

If you still want to spend a little money but keep things local, check out Facebook marketing. This is where you put an ad on Facebook that will show up specifically in the regions and demographics you are looking for. Facebook marketing can be done as cheap or as most expensive as you would like to go. There are plans for every price point and can be a good start at marketing to see what customers may think of your business off the bat.

If you have the available money, I always would suggest hiring an actual advertising firm for your business. You can easily check places out online, view their clients, results, etc. If you have the money available do not be afraid to ask for help. It could potentially be a big lifesaver and game changer in your business. Advertising firms are professional, know how to work with the dollars available to them and can help you create a great campaign you might not have dreamed possible.

I hope this gives you some idea of where to start for marketing. I know there is a ton of information that I did not include in this chapter, but you could literally write a book all about marketing on its own… oh wait, there are a ton of books already out there about it. Well, here is to some good reading if you want to continue on. Like I said in the beginning of the chapter, the first thing you need to come up with is a dollar amount you are willing to spend on marketing and advertising. The amount you choose will then guide you on the right path to what is best for you and your business.

Lesson 12: Your Elevator Pitch

The art of a pitch can come in many different forms. There are plenty of books and information out there that is readily available for you to read and take advantage of. So why are you reading this chapter? Your guess is as good as mine, but my guess is that you already bought the book, so you might as well read it, right? Well do not let me keep you. I cannot write your elevator pitch for you without knowing your business. What I can do in this book however is put a little list together of some good keys to follow for your elevator pitch.

One of the first things you need to ask yourself is what is the goal of your pitch? Are you looking for potential clients or investors to join your organization? You might be pitching a specific product or just trying to simply engage a few interested people to get some excitement in your business. It is not uncommon to have a few separate pitches ready in your arsenal for any situation that comes up. I would suggest at least two under your belt. The first would be a pitch to potential clients and customers. The second would be more investors or buyouts.

The second thing to find is a good and quick hook. Being able to grab a cusotmer or an investor's attention with an interesting hook can be one of the largest battles of the elevator pitch. Many investors will normally not take the time to read the business plan you spent three years researching and writing. Usually something funny or shocking is generally acceptable with any genre of your business. Whatever your pitch is just make sure that it is relatable to your audience.

The third key is to make sure you get your mission across in your pitch. Just by reciting your mission statement your listener should understand what your business is about and what you are trying to accomplish. For example; lets say that your mission statement is "creating a safe environment for kids in the evening time within major metropolis cities across the United States." With a mission statement like that your audience will know exactly what your business is and what your goals are in a simple sentence and more importantly in about five seconds when you say it out loud.

The fourth key is timing with your pitch. You never know how much time you will have with the right person. It may be as small as just 10 seconds, but you may get lucky and get about 60-90 seconds. Make sure you have a few different renditions of your pitch to fit the right time frame you have. This can be difficult for many individuals keeping a pitch within a certain time frame. Many of us, including myself at times, may try to shove in too much information into a "quick" pitch and end up running out of time or worse, just confusing your listener with too much information that they cannot comprehend. The key to understand is that if you have not grabbed your listener's attention within the first 12 seconds, there is probably not much worth going on for. If an investor wants to know more on something, they will ask. Be short and sweet, but not vague.

The fifth part is to create a closing that is unforgettable. You have already spent much of your days and years probably putting in the research and work for your business startup, so do not let it slip away in the final few seconds of a poor pitch to an investor. You need to think creatively and simply at the end, summarize your main points, or whatever main points you were able to rattle off in 60 seconds. Then close with an open ended question to help engage your audience to respond.

I have said many times when talking with people that you are only as strong as the people you surround yourself with. I would like to think that I am a fairly smart person, but I am also smart enough to understand there are more people out there that are smarter than I am. I would hope that you are smart enough to realize this fact as well, so that means that you have probably brought in a few smart people into your business and company and there is no shame in putting the names of those great people in your pitch. Investors are usually put at ease a little when they hear that your business has such great people helping you run things smoothly. Your team information within your pitch may be as simple as telling investors that you have a great team setup and ready to run. When you get into a situation where you can expand on your team, do not be afraid to work up your team to an investor. It puts their money at ease in many cases to know there is more than just one person (you) controlling things. Many investors will often tell you that a company's leadership can actually be more important than the actual business's idea. The fact is no matter what your business is; your business will die if you do not have the right people in the right place. Being able to recognize where your faults are will give you the ability to correct those issues. Never be bull-headed enough to believe that you can do everything yourself.

One last thing you need to think about is your one-sentence pitch. It is always good to have a 30 second and 60 second pitches at the ready because you never know when or where you are going to run into someone who is interested or that will at least listen to you. When you are at your next dinner party or get together with friends, family, or others… the question always will come up "so what are you up to these days?" Hence, this is where you would entertain them with a simple headline approach that should strike their curiosity to ask more. Then that is when you dive in a little deeper.

I hope this gives you at least a little insight into what it takes to come up with a great elevator pitch for your business. You can never practice enough in your preparedness. Do not be afraid to ask for help in writing your pitch. If you decide you want help, there are plenty of companies that will help write your elevator pitch for you. Do not be afraid to ask for help, but do not expect to get professional help for free.

Lesson 13: Sales

Even though this chapter is in the middle of the book, it is actually the last chapter I wrote for the book because there is just so much I could talk about on the topic of selling that I just did not know where to start, where to end, and what would be the best way to cover in such a short amount of time and space. Like many topics covered in this book, there are obviously books dedicated to these subjects and they are written by much more bright intellectual people than me.

How I am going to approach this chapter is that I am going to try and discuss some of the topics of becoming successful in sales. There are obviously more topics and ideas out there then what I am going to talk about, however the topics I will cover are what I feel are some of the more important ones in my personal opinion.

The first thing to understand is when to shut up. Obviously you need to introduce yourself to your potential customer, however there is no need to jump right in and start blabbing on about yourself, your products, your services, and for heaven sake, do not jump right into your sales pitch.

You have not have not even asked what your customer needs. You have no idea if what you are selling is of any use to your potential customer.

Trust, in my opinion, is the key to a successful sale and repeat customer. At the end of any business transaction, people only do business with people they like. A great salesperson has the flexibility to build rapport with anyone and establish a feeling of mutual likeness and trust every time a transaction is processed.

You must believe in what you are selling. Believing in yourself and also being able to take rejection is a key to any successful salesperson. Every salesperson deals with rejection in a positive manner. It is important to remember that even though a deal or transaction did not take place right now, laying down the foundation for a customer is never anything you should shy away from. If you believe your product or service is valuable and competitive, keep things in perspective and trust that the customer may come back in the future to check you out when they are truly ready to buy.

Sell your product with questions. Never ask a question you do not already know the answer to. Forget about trying to actually sell your product or service and focus your pitch on answering the question for your customer, why should I buy your product? For example let's say that we are trying to sell a music CD. You could probably talk for hours with people about the music, trying to describe what it sounds like or similar artists. This is you trying to "sell" the music. Instead, plug in some headphones and invite people to listen to the product. They will either like it or leave it. They will know within the first few seconds if it is something they will want to buy or not. Now you did not have to "sell" anything. The product spoke for itself and you did not even have to open your mouth other than to tell them how much the CD was.

Body language is a huge factor in being a successful salesperson. The ability to read a person's body language is a skill that not very many people have. What a person says does not always agree with what their body language is telling you. If you are someone that has the ability read body language well you can use this knowledge to help your sales pitch by being able to adjust your pitch to what you sense the customer may need to hear, feel, or see.

Always maintain a positive image with your business and yourself. Like we discussed earlier in the book, make sure your appearance is always professional. This also goes for your business as well. When anyone asks about your business, things are always going good. Do not advertise that your business is struggling. As far as anyone else is concerned, your business is going great and things are just peachy.

When you have to sell something, sell the benefits and not the features. As much as we would like to think that the general public is not selfish, that truth of the matter is that people care more about what your product or service can do for them rather than what you do with it. One great example is to compare the brochures of products and services with successful organizations and struggling ones. You will always notice a difference in presentation and that many of the successful companies talk about benefits of their products and services rather than features.

The follow-up is one of the most important aspects of creating a successful sale. Too many people believe that the sales process ends when you collect the payment. This could not be further from the truth. A follow-up can take as little as a 30-second phone call or even a quick email. Often, a follow-up can lead to an additional sale and up-sale, but if nothing else, you are showing your customer a level of service that many places do not offer anymore.

Well I think I have covered all of my more important thoughts on being successful at selling. There is definitely an art form to a good salesperson. Some people are born with the skill and others are not. It is definitely something you can teach, but it can take a long time even with the right person. Having the ability to sell a product or service is no small task and can benefit you greatly in your business. It is obviously something you will need if you want your business to be successful. No business will succeed just by opening its doors and if that is your plan, you would be wise to have a backup plan or at least a second job in mind.

Lesson 14: Starting at Break-even

This is probably one of the chapters that made me want to start writing a book like this. I have read and written many business plans in my short number of days. I've seen a lot of businesses succeed and a lot more fail, some that I have really loved and others that I could not wait to say goodbye to. Starting your own business in any way is no easy task, unless you have more money then you know what to do with, which if that is the case, why are you reading this book? One of the biggest flaws I see, in my personal opinion, within business plans and financial forecasts are the failure and determination to break even on the first day/month/year/etc. In my personal opinion, if you are not at least breaking even, then you are not succeeding.

Many small businesses and probably large businesses in that matter will tell you more times over that it is normal to not breakeven in your revenue and expenses for the first several months or even the first year. This is partly due to the fact that your business is new and you are still trying to get those new customers in to see what you have to offer. That is understandable and I do not fully disagree with the statement of not breaking in the first few months or first year. However, this is where my argumentative personality and stubbornness can take over and I start asking the questions why. Why are you not breaking even in the first month or 3 months or year, etc?

When I ask a new business this question, I get the usual answers like well we have so many startup expenses just like many other businesses, or I am spending this much on advertising in the first few months to help get the word out of the new business. There are always a few different answers but usually the same group of answers that a business owner will say when I ask this. I'm going to use a real life example for this section that I had to deal with when I started to help out on the business side of a new developmental sports team in the Hillsboro area, known as the Portland Boltz football team.

I offered my services to the team to do the business side of the football, helping with expenses, keeping track of money, etc, etc. I was also in charge of keeping the books with the finances of the team. It was the first year for the team and with any first year sports team, or business in this manner, you are going to have some initial costs of business. For a sports team, the two most expensive items on this initial list were gear for players and uniforms. To give you a general idea of the expenses, the uniforms cost about $3,000 for the team and equipment (helmets and shoulder pads mostly) ended up costing about $7,000 to get us started. For the actual business, these were asset purchases, which like equipment in your normal business can be depreciated over time. If you are unaware of the word, depreciation means that I can essentially write-off a certain percentage of the purchase over a period of time. So if I had $10,000 in equipment expenses, the business could actually write-off, for example, $2,000 of that equipment every tax year for five years. This is what is known as a straight-line depreciation for business owners. After 5 years, the equipment should essentially pay for itself and would need to be replaced by new equipment, hence starting the cycle all over again.

These types of initial expenses should not be included in what, in my opinion, I view as your basic revenue and expenses. For the example, think about your revenues as simple as possible; sales will probably be the simplest way to think of things. For my Portland Boltz example, it would be ticket sales, merchandise, and liquor sales. Those were their three main sources of revenue for the first year. As far as expenses for your small business, this could be items such as staff, electricity, rent, cost of goods, water, etc. For the example I am using of the Portland Boltz football team, our main expenses were stadium costs, officials, liquor, and staff.

Below is a breakdown of the first game's revenue and expenses:

REVENUE:

Ticket Sales:	$1,210
Liquor:	$205
Merchandise:	$80
TOTAL =	$1,495

EXPENSES:

Stadium Rental:	$1,300
Liquor:	$695
Merchandise:	$230
Officials:	$700
Staff:	$0
Advertising:	$300
TOTAL =	$3,225

NET AMOUNT = $-1,730 (NEGATIVE)

Obviously, as a businessman, I was not too impressed with our first game showing and was struggling to find the right words to say what I felt needed to happen. As an owner of a business, you can almost look at your business with blinders on through most of the way and not see changes that could be made to improve your bottom line as well as possibly improving your business both in the short run and in the long run. That is the case with the Portland Boltz. Owners were very stuck on keeping things a certain way and were not open to suggestions to make them more cost effective and with eventually the goal of at least breaking even and the larger expectation of actually making a profit.

My first suggestion after the first 2 games had a similar result was the change the venue of stadium to a more cost effective location. The stadium that was used for games was a state-of-the-art football stadium built by the City of Hillsboro Oregon on a huge sports complex. The rental rate for 4-5 hrs was the $1300 paid directly to the city. This included no staff for announcing, scoreboard, ticket booth, etc. Luckily the team found enough volunteers and people that were very interested in being involved to help out at no cost or a free ticket for their friends and family. Doing some simple research and calling around, I had found a football stadium that would have cost $80. This was a more local stadium in downtown Hillsboro. It was used mainly for high school football games, lacrosse games, and track events by the local high schools. The stadium expense was obviously one of the largest expenses for the team and one that I thought did not have to be as high at least in the first year as we started growing from scratch. It was my suggestion that the games be moved for the rest of the season, and what money you had left over, could have been used for advertising the event to sell more tickets.

My other suggestion was to hire a company to take over the liquor (beer) sales so you did not have to worry about staffing, paying liquor fees to the city agencies like OLCC, as well as worrying about the hiccups of security for drunk people at sporting events, which I am sure you can all imagine are just a pleasure to deal with on a nightly basis with summer football games.

My other suggestion was to take a look at the other expenses to see what we can do. With a third party coming in for liquor sales, you would have had to share a percentage of the profit, but for the sake of your sanity, sometimes it is easier to take a little less profit and not have to worry about it. For merchandise, it is quite simple that you just simply do not buy as much merchandise to sell and try to find that happy medium between how much you purchase and what you actually sell at your events. The officials cost we could not change as that was an agreement before the season started so those were a fixed cost. Advertising is another area that can be finely tuned as well. What and where are you spending your money on advertising? For the Portland Boltz, their advertising costs came from a single newspaper ad the week of the first game with a 2 for 1 ticket.

We talked about this in a previous chapter that advertising/marketing is a must do in some form of fashion for your business. You cannot expect to just open the doors and sit back to customers coming in. Unfortunately, those kind of small businesses are VERY hard to find and often do not stay small very long if they are that huge of a success. How you spend your marketing dollars is something you should be looking at constantly. Do not be afraid to spend a little money and try something out to see if it works. Often that is the best way to see what works for your business. For the Portland Boltz, the newspaper advertisement did not go over very well. When counting through tickets purchases, only a handful of newspaper ads were turned in for tickets, thus did not essentially "pay for itself" with the ad. At least paying for itself should be your initial goal with marketing and advertising your business. If your advertisement pays for itself with sales, then you are always at least one step in front of the game. For the Boltz, a similar 2-for-1 ad was placed on their team's Facebook page, which printouts of that particular ad were counted numerous times over and a huge success. The other added bonus with the Facebook coupon that was posted as a picture to the team page, it cost the Boltz $0 in advertising money.

Also remember that the picture advertisement of the 2-for-1 was put in the face of their direct customers. This is just another reason to have social media at your fingertips; free advertising directly to your customers at no cost. Let us look now at what could have been a break-even outlook of the first game had my suggestions been put into action and a few assumptions made on my part to what I believe would have happened had they followed my advice…

REVENUE:

Ticket Sales:	$1,480
Liquor:	$100
Merchandise:	$80
TOTAL =	$1,660

EXPENSES:

Stadium Rental:	$80
Liquor:	$0
Merchandise:	$230
Officials:	$700
Staff:	$0
Advertising:	$0
TOTAL =	$1,010

NET AMOUNT = $650 (POSITIVE)

As you can see there were some drastic differences with the expenses and a small increase in revenues with more of an impact in social media marketing with websites like Facebook, LinkedIn, Twitter, and Instagram.

Take a good look at your monthly operating expenses and revenues. Are you breaking even? Do you pay yourself a salary every month, is it too much (at least in the beginning could it be reduced)? If you are starting your own business, you may also have a full time job on top of things, so think about if you did not pay yourself as large of a salary and simply took a larger profit at the end of the month. It looks better for the business in the long run especially if you are looking for loans to expand later on. Make sure you look at EVERY single line of expenses and revenues you have, just like you might do on a monthly personal budget. You may have electricity setup in your budget as a flat $100 per month. It's safe to assume that your electricity bill is not exactly $100 every month, so where does that extra money go? My guess, as usual with most people, it goes towards a coffee in the morning or eating lunch out during the business week. I think the financial guru inside of me would have to say that extra $14.98 should go towards paying off your credit card, or paying more down on your car loan, etc, etc.

The bottom line, in my opinion, is that your business should ALWAYS AT LEAST be breaking even every month. Do not keep looking at your business with blindfolds on and like every expense is a fixed expense that cannot be changed. That is NEVER the case. Take a look and see if you are in that position. Are you breaking even? You should be. If not, shoot me an email and we can talk about things. Do not ever assume that you are breaking even every month. Take an actual look or let me come in and take a look, whether it is a business or a personal budget. Everyone and every business have a break-even point and you should be hitting it every month. If you are not, things need to change and fast for you to succeed.

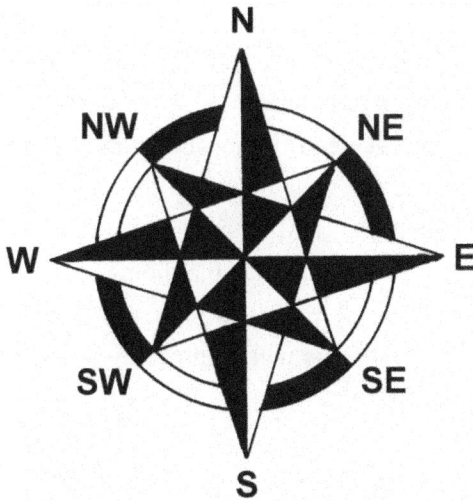

Lesson 15: Location Search

By now in your business you have probably started thinking about this at least a little bit. There are a lot of questions you need to think about when choosing a location for your business. The first, which you may have already decided depending on the business you are starting, is what kind of business you are going to have.

The first option is a business based out of your home. We are starting to see a lot of entrepreneurs start and even continue in their home till the point they cannot go on any further. There are definitely some big bonuses to using your house as part of your business. The first and most obvious is the cost of buying or renting space. If you have a spare bedroom, office, den, attic, etc and depending on the type of business you are running, a home-based business may be the right route to take. Some other key advantages to having your home as your business is that it cuts down on lease negotiations, deposits that may be needed for leasing a space out in the world, as well as commuting for work as well. I am sure the drive to your den is a lot faster then the drive at 7 AM on the freeway halfway across town for your normal job. Depending on the type of person you are however and how driven you can be, the home can often become a distraction for many business owners. The constant access to television, phone calls, and errands with everyday life can sometimes get in the way of your "9-5" work hours. A home-based business is also a good choice if the business only employs you. Having a variety of employees for your business that is out of your home can often become crammed and tight with no real room for physical growth of your business space. If you decide that home-based is the best choice for you, I truly recommend you creating a work schedule for yourself and holding yourself to it. This will help you avoid distractions that may come up throughout the day.

The second and most obvious is some type of retail business, which come in many different shapes and sizes as well as store fronts inside malls, and mix-use facilities. This is often the most popular choice for businesses if they cannot do a home-based business. The downfalls are unfortunately a part of everyday business with lease agreements, deposits, and even the opportunity to find a retail space that is within your budget. Going with retail can end up becoming the plague or stump that people never get over. The difficultness of finding a place that truly meets all your business needs at an affordable price can be harder then finding that perfect home.

A third option is keeping your business mobile, using your car, van, or truck as the main source of your business. This would make sense for businesses like plumbing services, maintenance workers, or other businesses where products or services are taken directly to the customer. Using and turning your personal car into a company car can be an easy transition and have some decent tax implications as well. Check with a tax professional about the proper way to "sell" your personal car to your business if that is something you are interested in. Using this third option may also tie in with a home-based business as well since major paperwork or files may be kept at your home office and not actually in the trunk of your 1998 Toyota Corolla.

The next two options are usually for more established companies or businesses that tend to need much more capital to startup. They include businesses for commercial and industrial. Commercial spaces would include things like actual offices, receptionist, etc. Industrial or manufacturing businesses will also be much more specific about where you could hold your business depending on the correct zoning and what your needs are.

When scouting locations for any business, there are many things to think about and research to try and find the most ideal place to give you the best opportunity for success. Check out demographic maps you can find for free online. These maps can tell you everything from how many people in households to how much the average household brings in for money and many other specific characteristics you may want to check out when looking at an area. Be smart about your choice. I would hope most people would be smart enough not to start an ice cream business next to a cemetery, but you'd be surprised what kind of ideas I hear or read about every day.

Scout your competition. If you are a restaurant of some type, take a look at your surroundings. Are there other restaurants around you? Maybe your choice of location is based on what businesses are around you like a college campus or large manufacturing company.

Entrepreneur Magazine put out a great list of questions in their December 2004 edition that I thought I would include in here for you to at least think about when you are looking for that dream location. Below are the ones from the list that I feel are most important:

1. Is the facility located in an area zoned for your type of business?
2. Is the facility large enough for your business?
3. Does it meet your layout requirements?
4. Does the building need any repairs?
5. Are the lease terms and rent favorable?
6. Is the location convenient to where you live?

7. Can you find a number of qualified employees in the area in which the facility is located?

8. Do people you want for customers live nearby?

9. Is the facility consistent with the image you'd like to maintain?

10. Is the facility located in a safe neighborhood with a low crime rate?

11. Is exterior lighting in the area adequate to attract evening shoppers and make them feel safe?

12. Will crime insurance be prohibitively expensive?

13. Are neighboring businesses likely to attract customers who will also patronize your business?

14. Are there any competitors located close to the facility?

15. Is the facility easily accessible to your potential customers?

16. Is parking space available and adequate?

17. Is the area served by public transportation?

18. Can suppliers make deliveries conveniently at this location?

19. If your business expands in the future, will the facility be able to accommodate this growth?

Those were just some of the top questions that I thought might be the most important to you when you are searching for a location. Like it is always said, one of if not the most important thing about your business is location, location, location.

Lesson 16: Staffing

Staffing your business can be an exciting time for most people. This is mainly because they get to choose who they want to work with. I am all for working with people you like and you enjoy being around, but do not underestimate the power of hiring someone you normally would not.

I had the opportunity to talk with a manager one time that was currently hiring for a position that people kept leaving to go onto larger things outside of this actual business. The position was a code enforcement officer for the police in a local city. We first talked about some adjectives that he looks for when looking at a resume or actually interviewing someone for this position. We put together a list of probably at least 20 and you could probably spend all day thinking of adjectives about a person that you would want in an employee. Cleanliness, resourceful, respectful, happy, on time, honest, and the list goes on and on of good qualities every manager looks for in an employee.

Then we took a look at the minimum qualifications which were pretty standard for a position of this type, which were a high school diploma and an interest in government or police work. To be honest, it does not take a PhD to drive around town and point out code infractions done by citizens. Many cities use interns from local colleges looking for credit towards a criminology degree. This job of code enforcement entailed just a little more office work within the police department as well as including entering ticket information and some small office management. It was an entry-level job with decent benefits for a public position. Well, to be honest, the benefits for most city government jobs are pretty sweet and it is the reason a majority of people work for the government.

After all that we took a look at the people that had been hired in the past for the position and why they were hired and more specifically why they chose to leave for another position outside the agency. After a couple quick phone calls to past employees and looking at applications it became quite apparent, at least to me, that all the employees loved the job, but a better offer came up with either greater pay or more responsibilities with all of the past employees having a great desire to move up in their career.

This is when the bell begun to strike in my head for the reason of such a fast turnover time between employees, at least for this specific position. Is it apparent to you? All the employees that were hired were of the younger generation and had a desire to move up quickly after finding a position. Once they received a decent amount of experience at the job, they started looking around and applying for that next step. You will find this characteristic in many millennials or also known as Generation Y (people born from 1980-2000).

We will talk a little more about this in the next chapter, but one common characteristic among Generation Y is they are usually less loyal to a certain company or brand specifically. Whereas older generations can often stay within a company for their entire career, Generation Y does not generally have a loyalty standard, which allows them the freedom of moving from one company to another, even if its switching jobs every 3-5 years.

When you look at starting to hire for your business, take a good look at what you need to succeed. Obviously you probably do not want to be hiring someone new all the time, but maybe you do want to keep hiring new people to keep the blood fresh as some may say. You need to identify what is needed in your business. Some general ideas to at least understand is that older generation employees may require a higher starting wage then many Generation Y or younger employees. The reason for this is because an older generation would generally have more experience in what you are looking for in your business.

Although an older generation may require a higher wage, this can also sometimes mean a cost-saver in the end because you will generally receive more loyalty from this person as they will not always be looking for the next great job path in their career and you will spend less time trying to hire a new person every few months. On the other hand, hiring a younger generation may be what you are looking for in your business as they usually bring a little bit a different view on how to do things and can often lead to easier or more technological ways of completing a process or specific task.

As most of us have in our lives, there are always certain processes we always follow, or habits, as I like to call these tasks. Habits form when you continue to do something for so long in the same way that you neglect to see an alternative and possibly more productive way of doing something. For some people, I like to call these habits the "old hag ways". Its not meant as a derogatory statement, but simply an identification of an old person getting stuck doing something a certain way. Someone new may come in to the process and see a more productive way of getting a task completed and it is important for all of us to take a step back even if we are the boss or manager and at least discuss what changes could be made to improve something.

When you look for an employee, are you actually matching the right job to the right person and characteristics? In the case mentioned above with the police code enforcer and office manager, would you hire another up-and-coming person or would you actually look for someone older who may not always be looking for that next step and is just looking for a steady job in their life? Try to match each job with the person who has the right characteristics to meet that job. Most positions in your business will likely not have available positions to move up within your business, as you most likely will only have a few employees specifically for your business to run things when you are not around.

Hiring the right person for your business can make your life either one heck of a mess or quite possibly the best choice you made in a long time. Having a staff that understands what needs to be done, when to do it, and how to do it, can take time to train. Make sure you show them by example yourself. Do not have another employee show them how to do something, you need to get your hands dirty too sometimes and show your employees that you still know how to get things done.

As you start working with you employees, do not hesitate to give them feedback both negative AND POSITIVE! Many managers are quick to point out faults and things that are being done incorrectly, but very few managers these days take the time to point out something an employee does correctly and a simple "thank you" or "great job" can go a long way to help make an employee feel more welcomed and appreciated. You do not always have to buy your employees gifts, but do not forget the act of kindness that can often go a long way and sometimes more then many physical gifts an employee may receive.

If you have employees for over a year, make sure you do an annual review with them of their position and let them know how they are doing. A yearly review can do a lot for you to show an employee they are doing a good job as well as show poor employees their performance standards and how they are not meeting them.

Having poor employees really falls into a Human Resources discussion, of which there are numerous answers to even the simplest of questions. My bottom line suggestion over this specific topic of poor employees is to make sure you keep your documentation about when you talked about with an employee about performance standards and create a roadmap or plan for that employee to help him achieve. With so many individuals these days quick to try a file a lawsuit against someone, always keep documentation showing what you have done to try and rectify the situation and how your interactions were with an employee of poor performance.

Lesson 17: Get To Know Us

There are a few things you probably should learn about people as you start looking at who you should be hiring for jobs within your business. There have been a lot of studies and people way more educated then me that could give you pages and pages of information about characteristics of people based on when they were born. In this chapter I will go through the three main generations and style characteristics of their general personalities. Please keep in mind that this information may be based on numerous studies, but be careful not to lump everyone in these categories. It should not surprise you that there are people out there in each generation that do not necessarily meet all characteristics exactly, so please try not to lump everyone and be prepared to find people that have better and/or worse characteristics then what is a generalization on their specific generation.

The first group to recognize is called Generation X. If you were born between the years of 1966 and 1976 then you could call yourself part of this generation. One of the great characteristics is that the group of Generation X individuals is actually the most educated of all our generations based on the US Census Bureau report. Often referred to as the "lost generation" because of a heavy increase on daycare and divorce and a need for attachment during these times in history, but this generation is also one of the first to truly be open and acknowledge characteristics such as race, religion, culture, language, and sexual orientation. Their increased dealings with divorce and broken homes when they were young often lead to more concerns about and caution about raising their own families and trying to avoid kids growing up without a parent around and sound financial planning.

The second group to identify, which is also my generation is Generation Y. If you were born between the years of 1977 and 1994 you are part of this generation. Since the baby boomers after the last World War, this is by far the largest populated generation. Often referred to as the Millenniums, Generation Y is generally more technology wise and actually more difficult to "trick" with old habits of advertising and marketing ploys by businesses. This stems from growing up more open and being exposed to more at a younger age then previous generations. One negative aspect of Generation Y is their problematic and more racially and ethical reservations. Generation Y is actually one of the more segmented generations. The old high school adage of staying within your group or social class tends to stay with Generation Y even after high school is over and the start into the real world begins. This generation generally has less brand loyalty then prior generations, which can stem from more availability of resources like access to the Internet and research capabilities. This generation is normally raised with dual incomes from both parents working full time or a single parent that creates more involvement in family decisions like with purchasing groceries and other large purchases like new cars and housing. It is also helpful to notice that this is the first generation to become financially responsible at the earliest age. That is, at least one in eight Generation Y kids had co-signed credit cards by the age of 18, giving them access to cash and credit at an early age… which can be great if it is used appropriately.

The third and most recent is labeled Generation Z. If you were born between the years of 1995 and Present (no specific date has been labeled yet) you would be under this generation. There is not a lot out there as far as generalizations for this group yet, but I am sure they will be out soon. One thing for sure is that this generation will be the most technological diverse group as they would have been born into the technology days of Facebook, Twitter, instant messaging, and the World Wide Web. How this will affect their generalization is yet to be determined and probably will not be visible for a few more years and the identification of a new generation, which has to be named as well. I am not sure what will come after Generation Z since they have reached the end of the alphabet. It was probably not the greatest of ideas to start with Generation X, since there are only a couple letters after it. We have Douglas Coupland to thank for the name of Generation X if you were wandering. He came out with a novel in 1991 called "Generation X: Talks for an Accelerated Culture". It was used sparingly before that to describe various different cultures that seem "different" because of their different then norm values.

There are also some prior generation characteristics but it did not seem necessary to go into too much detail about them. For those curious though here is a quick breakdown of the prior generations:

Depression Era ~ Born 1912-1912
World War II ~ Born 1922-1927
Post-War Cohort ~ Born 1928-1945
Boomers I / Baby Boomers ~ 1946-1954
Boomers II / Generation Jones ~ 1955-1965

So what is there to take from this chapter? Well I hope you learned a little history about history first off. If nothing else, you may be a little smarter and able to answer a few more questions when you play Trivial Pursuit now. What to truly take from this though are at least the generalizations about what you will get depending on who you hire for your positions. Like I mentioned earlier, it may be a great cost initially to hire someone in the Generation X mind, but generally speaking they are the most educated and can probably assist more in operations of your business and assistance. Hiring someone in the Generation Y area usually means you will get someone probably less educated and for that reason may cost you a little less in wages as well as giving you a little more assistance with a more technological aspect of your business. Take a few moments and think about what is needed for your business in particular and whom you think would be the greatest fit for your organization.

Lesson 18: Don't Discount – Add Value

We see a lot of businesses these days trying to use deep discounts to increase sales and eventually profit if they ever get there. The old ploy of steep discounts usually work in the short term generally speaking, but are usually not enough to create a stable business platform that is sustainable throughout the years.

Generally speaking when we walk into any store and see the big signs "SALE TODAY ONLY", it catches our attention and we usually at least take a quick peek. It is ok to admit, really. I am not ashamed that I shop a lot at the local Dollar Store. There are so many items there that I would generally be forced to buy at the local Fred Meyer or even Walmart, but it is important to not have the same expectations of a purchase at the Dollar Store compared to that of Fred Meyer or larger, more well established chain stores. Now this really depends on what you are buying.

Obviously I am not buying large ticket items at the Dollar Store... I am not expecting to see televisions and stereos and you should not either. It does nerve me a little bit though when I walk into large stores now and see things like toothbrushes or sponges "on sale" for $3.99 or buy one get one free at $4.99. I did not really shop at the Dollar Store until my wife and I were out on our own. Why would I buy a sponge for $3.99 from the local Fred Meyer, when I could purchase one at the Dollar Store for $1? I am sure there is a generalization and stereo type that goes with shopping at the Dollar Store, but I really just do not care if someone sees me shopping there. In fact, I actually invite people to my local Dollar Store because I am very proud of the large selection of items that you could be saving instead of purchasing even at the local Walmart. Saving even $1 to $2 on each item you purchase can end up savings you a ton at the end of the month or even the year. How much do you pay for toothpaste? If you shop at the local Walmart or Fred Meyer you are probably looking at least at spending $2 if not in the $3 range. I buy the same toothpaste as you, but I spend $1. Same brand, same size, just not the same price. There is no shame in that. I just feel sorry for you, but now you know and knowing is half the battle in life, so you are welcome.

Having the Dollar Store is great, but it is also important to keep your expectations in line as well. Like I mentioned before, I do not expect much in return for an item at the $1. Heck, I can buy my pots and pans from the Dollar Store if I wanted, but I know the quality is not great. I am not going to the Dollar Store for great quality though, I am there for one reason and one reason only... to save money. For many things we purchase though, like larger ticket items, and more specifically items that I purchase from your business, I may be looking for something a little more. This is where your sales skills come into hand that we discussed earlier in the book.

Many stores are quick to discount an item 10% here or there to help earn your business the first time and hopefully earn your thought process next time you think of something to buy and go to their store first. Like I mentioned at the beginning of this chapter though, this is only a temporary solution and will not help sustain you for a long-term business.

To be sustainable for the long term you have look at adding value to your products and dare me to say, keeping your current and regular prices. Like the lesson title suggests, do not discount your items, but instead add value to what your customer is purchasing. Let's use a quick example. Recently my father wanted to try a new BBQ restaurant that was located in downtown Portland. We live on the outskirts or suburbs of Portland, which ends up being about 25-40 minutes away from downtown Portland depending on traffic. So picture for me the 25 minute drive (best case scenario) to the restaurant and then the 10-15 minutes at the restaurant and then finally the 25 minute drive back to our house to eat the meal; all said and done we are looking at about a full hour trip just to try a new BBQ restaurant we had heard about from a friend (note to the reader; word of mouth marketing, just thought I would point that out to you). When the restaurant finished his order and heard that it was our first time there and even drove as far as we did to specifically try it out, she included a free desert item for the drive time. This added value to the order we were already going to purchase. The desert item was some kind of piece of cake that was absolutely divine at the end of our meal.

If you are a restaurant owner, you already know that the most profitable aspects of your business are appetizers and desserts, so the item we received could not have cost more than a dollar or two at most for the restaurant, but the added value was at least the retail price of it, which I would have to guess to be at least $4.99 if not a few dollars more, as like I said, it was divine. The meal was great in itself, but having the dessert at the end made us want to go back even sooner to try more and different items on the menu.

By adding value to your already regular priced item, you increase the value of that regular priced item. Another great example that may be more commonly used in cities with sports teams are season ticket packages for your local sports team. I am going to use a new local AAA-baseball team that just recently opened their first season. Their normal ticket prices for a regular season ticket range from $7 General Admission to $16 for individual reserved seating tickets. Obviously they have season ticket packages available. Most people who do not buy season ticket packages for sports would expect to usually see a discount on the per-ticket price, but for most sports teams, this is not usually the case. Ticket prices are usually kept the same to what the individual price would be, but the season ticket packages come with some extra benefits you would not normally receive.

Some of those benefits of the local baseball team include the same seats for all home games, first priority renewal, specific gifts for only season ticket holders, exclusive events throughout the year, early entry, personalized service, online management tools, and a few more added bonuses depending on what ticket level you purchase at.

Most of these extra items offered do not cost a whole lot for the team to add on as a benefit. There is no true cost to giving first priority for seat renewals, online management tools for customers, or having the same seats throughout the season, but all of these aspects add an intrinsic value onto the season ticket prices, which remember are the same price as buying individual tickets.

Deep discounts can also have a more negative effect on your products and services as well. Depending on the product or service, with a deep discount of 50-70% off that I see oh so many times throughout my shopping escapades, sometimes I find myself as a consumer asking if this item is discounted so much, is it really worth even purchasing? There is usually some thought process that goes on in all of our minds that if something is too cheap, it is almost not worth purchasing.

Let's look at one more example that I personally had a hand in working at a prior job. I worked for several years at Nordstrom starting out as a stock boy and helper during summer and winter sale times during college. After college I was offered a sales position when I completed school and was quickly moved into an assistant manager position within six months, then a full manager's position within the next year. As a department manager at a smaller store, I implemented a few different aspects that Human Resources and sometimes even the store manager was not a huge fan of initially until I had to explain myself of why I decided to do things a certain way.

The first was scheduling between my department which had myself and two other sales people that had been there working for quite a while once I first stepped onto the job. After closing one night, I took both out for food and drinks for the purpose of getting to know them a little more, what their goals are, and what they want to do. It was important for me to understand what my salespeople needed. One salesperson was fine just working their job every day and living life. The second salesperson was interested in moving up eventually and would like to become a manager one day himself. Just from a simple conversation I knew then what their goals were and I spent a little more time working with the one that wanted to move up and helped him learn what he needed to know and what I could teach him from my experience in the business thus far. This process of just simply talking with your employees about their future gave them an intrinsic value about their positions. It let them know that I was not just their manager and boss, but also someone they could reach out to if they wanted to improve something or talk to me about something specific.

The second thing that was changed was scheduling. This is where HR and the store manager stepped in for the first time. I was approached by one of salespeople about the desire to take some weekend classes. It required them to be at school during Saturdays and every other Sunday. When he approached me about the course, I talked with him about what the classes were for and why he wanted to take them. I could sense he had a passion for what he wanted to take the classes for and it seemed important to him. I adjusted the schedule for the next 3 months to take his request into consideration and scheduled myself and the other salesperson (which I spoke with as well) to work more Saturdays and Sundays. Human Resources and the store manager saw the schedule changes and at first questioned me about not having him working on Saturdays, which most salespeople see as the largest day of the week for shoppers. I had to explain to the HR manager and the store manager that as long as the classes were something that he wanted to do, myself and the other sales person agreed to the changes, and if his sales stay at least the same or improve... why should they care? I initially saw HR and the store manager conversation as an attempt the micro-manage my department and I was not afraid to speak bluntly to them explaining my thought process and finally asked the HR and Store Manager why I was a manager if I was not allowed to manage my department. This all happened in the first month of my job starting there, so I personally think a little power play attempt started before I squashed it to pieces right then and there. After the conversation, I had no issues or questions with my scheduling from then on.

The third thing that I changed after a few months of working eventually changed a little bit of the company as well, but something I am not sure I can take 100% credit on. So lets get that straight before I go on. At my local store, we had a large amount of business traffic from a neighboring office building and the lunch hour was one of the largest selling sixty minutes of the day during the business week. Being such a small department though, meant not always having the exact size I needed in a shirt for a customer or not having an item at all they saw at the same store, just across town. One of the downfalls of a small department and store is that buyers generally do not give you all the products that other stores may have in stock regularly. If we did not have a shirt in the right size or something like that, we had to offer to ship the item to the customer at the shipping cost of $4.95 or transfer the item in from another store. Most customers took the free choice of transferring the item in from another store, but after we would get the item in and contact the customer, the actual pickup rate was less than 20% of all the items we actually transferred in. One day I went ahead and made a judgment call as I was tired of seeing items transferred in for my department and thinking about the cost of actually transferring stuff from as far as the other side of the country at another store, I went ahead and instituted a department policy of offering to ship the item to the customer for free, taking away the $4.95 fee for shipping. We saw an immediate turnaround in our sales and a huge drop in our transfers into the store, which essentially cut costs from shipping items in from other stores. We continued this policy until I left the store about a year later and ended up leaving retail all together to try my hand at a normal 9-5 job and actually use my accounting and business degree. Now, Nordstrom offers to ship items to you with no shipping costs, adopting my prior departmental practices. Like I said before I started the story, I cannot officially take credit for this change in policy as the company standard, but I would like to at least say I was the first in the company to start offering it. Where it went after I left the company, I have no idea. But if you are a shopper of Nordstrom, you are welcome on my behalf if it means anything.

As you can see from my examples, both did not discount the actual items they were selling, but instead added value aspects to the product that made the item seem like it was worth more to the customer. Adding these little values (that should cost your company little if nothing at all) gives your customer a sense of product responsibility and also shows that you stand behind your product. As a business, you can always be on the lookout for cheap ways you can add value, because this whole process is about adding "perceived" value. As a general rule, try adding values based on the actual price value; for example, a more expensive item would receive more perceived value than those at a lower price. One very easy way of adding a "perceived" value is to focus your sales pitch on the benefits and quality of your product instead of the actual price.

Giving away products or services to make it look like your customer is getting a greater value for their money is an option as well, just make sure you are not losing actual money on those products. The extra you are offering should have cost you little if not anything for you to provide. Something as simple as offering the customer to choose a custom color on a product can do the trick, giving them the opportunity to personalize what they are purchasing from you. It is not what you give away, but how important and valuable your customer believes it to be. Take a few minutes and think about what perceived values you can offer for your business.

Lesson 19: Find a Coach

Everyone needs a little help sometimes throughout their life. You just cannot do everything yourself, as much as some people would like to believe they can. We will talk a little more about time management and overworking yourself in a later chapter, but for right now I would like to focus on some tools and people that might be able to help you achieve your goal or at least make it more successful.

There are several different ways to take a look at this topic and certainly many different roads you could take, if you feel that you might need a little help with your new business idea. The easiest and most common way to find someone to help is to look right beneath you, whether it is a friend that has the ability to help you out with ideas of their own on how things should happen or even just a difference of opinion that can sometimes be very helpful. For some it may be a family member that you have talked with before and seems interested enough to help you along the way in a variety of different areas. For people out in the world that do not seem to have anyone to talk with about their idea, the option may come down to actually purchasing help in some form of a business coach.

It is very easy these days to jump on the Internet and search around the world for business coaches. Most are very eager to take your money and give you a few, if any, decent ideas at all. Needless to say there are a lot of scammers out there looking for anyway to make a few bucks from you and others out there. To show you the worst case scenario, I am reminded of an article I read back in January of 2013 about a company called Ivy Capital, which was originally an online business that sold programs, products, and services as assistance to business owners who needed help or coaching. These services ranged anywhere from $2,000 up towards $20,000 for premium packages. In January 2013, an article was released after the federal Trade Commission announced that the company was officially accused of taking more then $100 million from entrepreneurs who received very little in return and also found it very difficult to get a refund once they decided to cancel their services. The company eventually agreed to settle with the Federal Trade Commission pleading guilty to misrepresenting their coaching programs, products and services and also failed to disclose their return policy, which is actually a federal law. The business surrendered all of the business's assets as well as two homes and eight cars. Customers will probably see very little in return compared to what they paid originally when they signed up for the program.

If you are someone who is actually looking at doing something like this where you purchase time for a business coach, there are a few simple things and FREE things you can do to check out someone you are thinking of using. The first is to look at their history as an advisor and look to see who and what companies they have advised, looking out especially for their experience with startups and small business owners. There is a big difference between a coach for a large corporation and a coach for a small business. The second thing to look at is the person's credentials. You do not necessarily need any special license to become a business advisor, but they would usually have some sort of business school experience, like an MBA, CPA, or professional certificates of various types. The third is to try and find a coach that specifically has experience in your field. There is no sense in getting a coach with only retail experience if you are in the technological field. Finding a coach within your field may also help you find more assistance and possibly capital with connections that your business coach may have from his experience in your field. There are several legitimate websites out there that can help you find a good business coach.

Here are a few: (www.score.org) (www.wabccoaches.com) (www.businessadvisor.com). The last thing to remember is that it is always a good idea to ask for references, but remember this, asking for references is no different than putting references on your resume. You would never put down a reference that was going to give you a bad review. You are going to put the best of the best references down and that is no different than what you will receive from a potential business advisor.

Lesson 20: Embrace Failure

I remember very distinctly from so many business classes and so many interviews with small business owners and others that have seen success in their businesses as well as failure and one thing was always a constant comment or answer when we discussed the topic of failure. The answer was pretty simple, you are going to fail. Then you will fail again and again. 99% of us will get things wrong the first time around and probably the second time around as well. It is nothing to be ashamed about and nothing that should also put you off on starting your own business.

We all pretend to listen to our parents when we are teenagers or in our 20s when they are giving us advice. We all pretend to listen to our college professors with years of experience and more education then many of us would dream of sitting through. It is ok because our parents did the same thing to their own parents and our professors did the same thing when they were in college as well.

The failure of a business does not tend to be something many of us like to admit. It is also usually something that happens over time. With the failure of a business, we usually wake up one morning and realize we cannot afford to pay groceries, you are out of money, up to your ears in debt and you start to think to yourself, how did it get to this point? This is the first step in creating success out of your failure.

For many businesses that fail, the process of trying to find what went wrong can be a very eye-opening experience. Many business owners start by making a small concession in something somewhere in their business. Paying more then you could truly afford in your budget for rent or hiring too many employees. Just like a new credit card owner, the extra expenses start to add up and can come up quickly when the bills start to come in.

Turning a failure into a success can mean a number of different things to different people. To me, I take it as starting fresh with a new idea. Learning from the mistakes that I made in prior business opportunities and hopefully not making the same mistakes I made originally.

I have four simple ideas for you to think about when failure occurs. The first is to try not to make excuses. Many people are quick to try and blame their failure on other people. It is ok that you made mistakes, we all make them. No one is perfect, not even you or me. The second is to not pretend it did not happen. Many business owners are quick to cover things up and try to avoid the conversation that comes along with the failure of a business. Denying that your business existed or failed will never give you the ability to look back and see what lessons you were taught and will also consume your thoughts throughout the upcoming nights. Do not be afraid to admit your failure. The third is to not confuse your failed business with you as a failed person. Just because your business fails does not mean you are a failure. The fourth and last thing you need to remember is that you are never alone. Businesses fail ALL the time in this world. Many businesses fail even before reaching a grand opening.

The main point I am trying to make with this chapter is to never give up on your dream, even if you fail the first seven times. As long as each time you are learning something from your mistakes then you are on the right path. I do not joke when I say that many millionaires today have failed more then they have succeeded in business. Never be afraid to fail. Failing only means that you tried and did not succeed. Many people that have a dream never even get the opportunity to fail because they never try.

Lesson 21: Eliminate Distractions

I have lived with a motto all through my life and it has really helped me keep a focus on what is important and especially who is important in my life. I am sure all of you have situations that happen in life that stress you out, may have caused you pain in someway emotionally and physically, or that have just been such a large distraction in your life that your business and/or personal life ended up feeling neglected.

This is probably the part of the book that you could consider the self-help section. Some of you may find my method unnerving and tactless, others who studied philosophy or psychology may have another type of description that you believe stems from something that happened in my childhood that I still have not overcome. My answer to those people would be yes, you are probably correct. This method I live by was brought on by my childhood, and as cruel as it may sound at times, it has proven itself handy when the time comes in a relationship of any kind both business and personally.

The method is called, Mutual Contribution. In any successful personal relationship there is a give and take between partners. Whether we are talking about a couple dating or married or even just friends between two guys or two girls, it does not matter. What I am talking about is any type of relationship between two people, hence the word "Mutual".

Those that had the pleasure of knowing me when I was a young child know some of the things that I had endured from the age of when you could talk to about the middle of college. I had a birth defect that was one in a million. In a nutshell without any of the scientific words and mumbo jumbo, it was a birthmark on my entire left ear that was completely red, making my ear completely red like it was getting ready to burst with blood. When I hit puberty, it actually started to grow and became large enough that my family and I were fortunate to find a specialist doctor in Denver Colorado that was the only person in the world at the time that had dealt with cases like mine and could correct the issue. Starting in high school, my parents and I would travel from Portland, OR to Denver, CO EVERY 6 WEEKS for surgery on my ear. The surgery would entail them injecting ethanol alcohol into my blood veins in my ear that the doctor could pinpoint exactly which ones to kill and which ones to leave alone. After 32 surgeries was one large reconstructive surgery done by a specialist in Denver as well. He took a few hours and extra cartilage from my ear to reshape my entire ear to look normal and what you see today. Sound fun? I didn't think so. But I digress; needless to say, I had a few select friends during my school days that I could truly call my friends. That has carried on throughout my life and I am still friends with that core initial group to this day.

Having this defect in my life, taught me many valuable lessons in life that I still use to this day. I learned from a very young age whom I could trust as a friend and who was not a friend. It also taught me to have tough skin when I was made fun of, humiliated, or any other sort of thing you can think of if you were one of those kids getting picked on. I could have very easily been one of those kids that had gone crazy and done something bad, but my family and life at home was what kept me sane and I truly believe without my family and core group of friends, I would not be here today.

Over the years I have seen friends come and go and I have enlisted this method on a few other people in my life when they have faced certain obstacles and I am glad to say that it has worked in some form or another to solve the problem. Friends and sometimes even family can become a very stressful problem in everyone's lives at some point and it can happen repeatedly as well. How we (you) react to these situations is completely up to you though. You control how you react to situations and how you feel. You can control whom you do not like and whom you like, whom you love and whom you hate. The choice is truly up to you.

To be straight and honest with you, letting others get underneath your skin is not the other person's problem, it is yours. Let me give you a simple example that I have used in my personal life. I had a "friend" that I had known for a couple years. During college we were roommates for about two and a half years. He seemed like a great guy during that time, until he left and the world seemed a little calmer around college and our dorms. In college I had 3 roommates total (so 4 guys total sharing a living space and kitchen with 2 bathrooms). All 4 of us also hung out with a neighbor group of girls. Let's get one thing out of the way and explain there was no funny business amongst anyone, we ended up all just being friends during our time at college.

In college was when I started drinking and during my junior year, was when I drank the heaviest. My girlfriend (and current wife) would often point out how much I was drinking, but I did not take much notice of it since it was always happening around me. Little fights and arguments would break out every now and then especially with my bathroom roommate. Now thinking back, I cannot remember much of what the arguments were of, so obviously they must have been super important at the time (can you sense my sarcasm?). Halfway through my junior year, this friend graduated early and ended up leaving all of us to go back home and start his own life. When he left, it was a drastic change in our dorm rooms and with the overall feeling between our two groups of males and female friends. Suddenly there were no more fights, everyone was getting along with each other and my bathroom roommate and I actually became good friends throughout the rest of our college careers. It took my wife to point out to me that all of these changes happened when that one person left and the dynamic changed for the better along with the constant drinking. This got me thinking about how I have actually used this similar method throughout my life when I just simply "cut people off" and ended relationships between other people.

As most all of you should know, a relationship or friendship has to be built on giving and taking. Each person in the relationship has to give and take and should do so equally throughout the relationship. If one person is always taking (complaining) and the other person is always giving (listening) then the relationship is always going to be one sided and will never truly be a fruitful one and lasting one. I am sure all of you out there can think of one person that is constantly complaining about something and never really takes the time to listen to your problems when you need to vent. We all know someone like that in our lives. So what would happen if you cut that person off? How much less stress would you have in your life? How much more time would you have to spend with the people who love you and how much more time could you devote to your business and life? That is what you need to think about.

I have told this method to many of my friends, in which they usually reply with the question... So you just cut them off completely? The answer is yes, I do. Isn't that a little harsh? Yes, it is. Is it hard to deal with when you do that? Sometimes, yes. The net effect however, always outweighs the stressfulness of having to deal with that person. As time goes by, you may feel like reconnecting with that person. It is fine to do that, but be careful not to get stuck in the trap again. As much as people like to say they have changed or that people change from who they were in high school... they really do not. The popular kids will still act popular. The jocks will still act like jocks. It's similar to one of my favorite sayings in business; Meet the new boss, same as the old boss. I love that line every time I hear it because it reminds me of my own motto; Mutual Contribution.

Try using this motto in your daily life when things get too stressful and it seems like there is not enough time in the day. What is truly important to you and are you getting a mutual contribution from that thing or someone in your life? By eliminating distractions of things and people that take up your valuable time, you now how an extra 30 minutes here or couple hours there to do something more productive rather then listen to your co-worker's complaints about how her husband never cleans dishes or picks up and they always fight. I am sure you can think of something better to be doing then listen to that. Give it a shot and you will be surprised about how much more time you have in your day and in life, especially with your life being less stressful as well.

Lesson 22: Build or Join a Network

In my personal opinion, building a network of customers, clients, and friends is no different then a different approach to marketing yourself as a person. Just like you go out and meet new people at events or gatherings, building a network of clients for your business are no different.

When your business first gets going, depending on what it is, you should always start things off with a bang, whether this is a grand opening party at your store or if you are an online service holding an event at a local establishment and inviting everyone you know.

Every single person is a possible future customer or client. Think about how many friends each of your friends have and so on and so forth. It is not much different then the old pyramid selling schemes we see all over the place these days. You get one person to join, and then they bring three friends along. Then those three friends bring three more friends along and so on and so forth. The scheme has been around as long as dirt. Many of us at some point in our lives have probably worked for something similar if not the exact type of business. These are the late night infomercials and daytime commercials that promise riches upon riches working part time and from your own home without using any of your own money. It's all right; we have all been there and fallen for it.

Take advantage of as many free networking sites as you can. The most popular ones will be Facebook (via your personal page or business page), Pinterest (making pins/posts about your business), LinkedIn (creating a profile for yourself and making as many connections as you can), and Twitter (making posts about your products and services). Also check out your local business associations available in your city. Although joining is usually not free, they can provide essential network gatherings and a multitude of events for your business to attend and meet potential clients. ALWAYS make sure you have a handful of business cards with you at any time. Do not be afraid to leave a card or two on your table at the food court or even in the bathroom. You would be surprised how many calls you may get from that one. What else is there to do when you are in the bathroom doing your business, you might as well take a quick glance at a business card and see if something strikes your interest.

When you are online as your business, make sure to comment on posts, but be respectful. Opening the lines of communication can lead to ongoing discussions about anything and creating a trustworthy networking client for your business. When replying online to someone's post, do not just write a quick two-word reply. Make it meaningful and engaging. Take the 20 seconds and actually look at the job history of a new client or customer. One of the largest mistakes I find with businesses and people as well is their willingness to scorn other businesses. Although you may have a personal opinion about a certain business or company, try to refrain from flaming people or businesses. Doing so looks bad on your part most of all, especially when outside people are looking at your company and may take offense to something you write or take something the entirely wrong way that is written.

When writing posts on websites make sure to reread what you have written and make your post is as clear as possible. The poor result of anything written on the Internet is that many of the things you write can be taken in many different impressions. It just depends on how the reader chooses to read and interpret what you are saying. So choose your words carefully.

Social networking sites offer people that may be a bit shyer and socially awkward more of an opportunity to network in a less dramatic alternative as opposed to a typical networking event in person. But you should never stop at just online networking.

As socially awkward you may believe yourself to be, there are definitely situations where you need to push yourself to get out there more and make yourself known around the community. Bring a friend or co-worker if that helps you, but do not rely solely on online networking to give you all your business.

In life, who you know really does matter. Relationships are what businesses thrive on and what will help you succeed and grow from the beginning till the end.

When trying to network out in person, there are two important things you need to learn and learn how to do well. The first knows how to approach people; and total strangers at that. Many people have boundaries, so try not to overexert yourself and make the situation uncomfortable. Give someone you are meeting the first time a good excuse to remember you. As much as none of us like to admit, we all make assumptions about someone when we first meet them. Even as much as I hear people talk about never judging someone before they meet or not basing an opinion on one simple meeting, it is just a bunch of crap. You have about five seconds to put down a good impression when meeting someone for the first time, so make it count. It is unfortunate but true that it can take almost a life time to change someone's opinion of you if it is poor on your first encounter.

The second part of great networking is being able to follow up afterwards. This is usually the part where many people fail for a multitude of reasons from laziness, to well; laziness is about the only excuse and what it all boils down to.

Following up is where using technology can really come in handy. It may not be the easiest option for you to call and follow up with every single person you meet in a single night. It is, however, more then easy to write a single email. Even if the email is just thanking to meet them and exchanging contact information. You must ALWAYS follow up with a new client or potential customer you meet. Maintaining contact with your customers through even weekly posts on Facebook about your business or maybe an article you write once a week pertaining to your business in some way. It does not matter, as long as you are maintaining contact through any of these free tools available for you to use. Doing so will ensure that your time will not be wasted and it keeps the potential for doors to open later on down the road.

Lesson 23: Do Not Overwork

This lesson was written because of the better half in my life. If you are married or have a long standing and serious relationship, understand that taking on a business can be more then a full time job. For most business owners, it is hard to "switch" the off button when you are not at work. That is also the case for many hard workers like me. I was born and raised with the notion that hard work and determination will pay off. As much of that is true, it is also sometimes difficult to learn how to balance life and work. For many of us, we bring our work home with us. Maybe not physically if you are one of the lucky ones, but something is almost always on your mind about work; whether that is something like a report that is almost done and you keep thinking about things to change or add to it. Or it could also be a work relationship that has gone bad and it is stressing you out.

In Europe (specifically France), once every year, residents take part in a time-honored tradition known as 5-week vacation. In a nutshell, workers are granted 5 weeks of vacation every year to take off and do whatever they want. It's basically a guaranteed and mandatory vacation. For Americans, the notion of even taking 5 days off in a row may seem like the most foreign of concepts, but the benefits are definitely there. Most notably, the benefits of getting away from it all for a decent amount of time (at the very bare minimum of 1 week), is more quality time with your family and healthier and happier children who do better at their schooling.

Another concept that MANY Americans need to get over is that most of us truly believe that without you at work, the company you work for will crumble to its knees and beg you to come back. I am sorry to be the one to say this to you if you have not heard it before, but if you get fired from your job or you decide to leave on your own accord, the company you used to work for will go on. Life will go on without you at work. Yes, maybe a few invoices will be late, paychecks may be late a day, or an error might come up every now and then… but overall, life will not cease to your pleasure. You are not as important as you believe you are in your job. So why are you giving up everything for your job?

Similar choices need to be made about your new business as well. Like I stated before, owning your own business is one of the toughest and longest jobs of your life and if you choose to take this job on, it can be very difficult to step away even for a couple days. I understand, it is your baby and it has been with you since conception. It is ok however, to take a step back, and see if the business can operate without you there 24 hours a day. If you have done things correctly, you should not have a problem stepping away at least for a little rest and relaxation and some much needed time with you family.

Lesson 24: Create a Roadmap

Creating yourself a business roadmap is something most of us think about in our heads, but probably never put down on paper. I suggest you try it. Putting your goals down on paper and leaving them in plain site will help keep you motivated to reach that goal. You can make this task as simple or complicated as you want. Just remember to use tactics and ideas that work for you and your business both financially and that are accessible to you.

We would all love to put down a goal of becoming a millionaire. I am not ashamed to admit it is one of my goals, but how we get to that point can be different from person to person. For most of us, becoming a millionaire is a matter of just playing the lottery. For others, it may be a step-by-step process of 30+ life long steps with the ending goal of becoming a millionaire. This is where your personality really comes into play.

For your business goals, think both short term and long term. I did a similar process for my goal of writing this book. Each week, I set a specific number of chapters that I wanted to complete. I kept the goal realistic and feasible as well. That is another key. Make sure your goals are achievable.

Your business might start out with a goal of having 100 "likes" on Facebook within 2 months of creation. That is a great goal. The next step in creating a roadmap is to actually write down what you are going to do to achieve that goal. Whether it is spending money on Facebook advertising or simply inviting friends from your personal account to like the page, it does not matter. Like many things in life, it may not make a huge difference in what you do, but how you do it that matters.

Although everyone's roadmap will be a different, there are always some key elements that you should always identify. Some of those standards will include reinvestment, growth, and financial targets. Each of these sections may include specific goals that you intend to reach within a certain time frame in your business. It may be more helpful trying thinking backwards. First you identify your goal, and then you write about how you are going to achieve it.

It can be important for your employees to buy-in to the roadmap and also identify your goals so they can help you achieve them. One of your goals may be to have no bad customer comments in your first six months of being open. Now how are you going to achieve that? A few strategies may include things like always thanking the customer, trying to learn each customer's name that comes in, or also by following up with each customer that comes in to make sure they were satisfied with their shopping experience and the item of purchase.

You and your employees should be able to see the roadmap and strategies throughout the day, so make sure it is posted in a visible area so it is a constant reminder. It will help employees to understand their daily tasks, requirements, and expectations as they help you achieve success.

Do not be afraid to review your goals as little as every month, every quarter, every year, etc. There is no limit to what you can set your goals up to be. If you want to focus on small monthly goals, that is great. Just revisit your roadmap every month to make sure you are meeting your goals. Do not be afraid to change your goals, just make sure your employees know what you are changing and why you are changing it.

What happens if you do not meet your goals? It is nothing to worry about yet, but you need to take a close look at why you did not meet your goals. Were they too far of a reach? Remember to make your goals feasible and accessible. Was there a clear channel to reach your goal? Did you identify the strategies and process to reach that specific goal?

Many businesses will run into problems when they spend too much time trying to make circumstances fit their plan rather then change their plan to fit the circumstances. Let me give you a quick example my thought here. For my consulting business, I set everything up and my pricing for services so that I could cater to small businesses and personnel service. I already had a full time job and family so being able to go out and network people was difficult to do at times. Instead of using this circumstance negatively and forget about actually marketing to businesses, I made one of my strategies to contact by person, email, or phone, one new small and local business each week. This kept my goal of one business feasible and manageable with my busy schedule. In this case, as you see, I simply changed my networking strategy to fit my circumstances.

It can be very important for business owners to actually create a roadmap for their business. Thinking and remembering goals in your head is great. The problem you will have, as you will find out, is that in your head, many of your goals tend to get laid by the waste side or changed without anyone who works with you knowing. Having to physically right your goals and keeping them in a visible area will be a constant reminder for you and keep you on track to reach those goals.

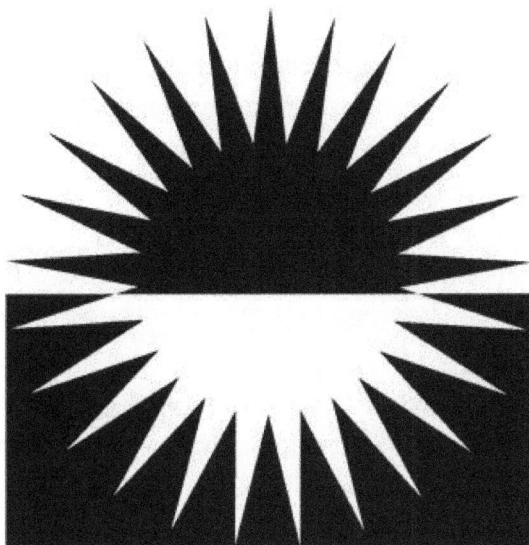

Lesson 25: Be Creative

It is important to remember that in owning your own business, you are the boss and you are free to try anything you want and be as creative as you want. Do not be afraid to try something that has never been done or something that you truly believe in. You can usually find a lot of new and creative ideas on websites like Pinterest. Pinterest is a growing website that many individuals are already using and businesses are starting to creep up as well to help introduce new products or concept ideas. Social websites like Pinterest can be an essential tool for any small business and like other social websites is easily able to track to see how your "pins" or posts are doing in comparison with others.

This is probably at least one of the reasons you started your own business; so you could do what you want when you want and how you want. There is no one to answer to whether it is right or wrong other then yourself, right? Well that can be a good and bad thing depending on the result of your creative idea. The blaming game does not work too well when there is only one person.

I remember when I was younger and both my brother and sister were already in college. My dad woke up one morning and found a blown up can of coca-cola in the freezer. His first thought, obviously, was to come get me. There was not anyone else to blame so why not, right? Now that did not stop me from trying to pin it on anyone but me, but the only other people in the house were my mom and dad, so I did not get very far on that one.

Customers are a great source to see what they are looking for or enjoy. They are your purpose, so getting ideas about what they want to see is great. Like we have talked about, it is up to you to take those ideas and figure out what would work best for you, but do not be afraid to go straight to the source as these are the people you are trying to get into your store or business, is it not?

Now being creative does not just mean trying to get people into your business, but you can also get creative with your expenses. Actually what I should say is there are almost always a few different ways to split a buck, so do not be afraid to try something and see how it works.

For example, look at your fixed costs, like rent for example. Are you on time with you rent, a great tenant, and overall bringing success to the area around you? Maybe your landlord is willing to negotiate a lease reduction for your slow times during the year and higher during the busy times like Christmas. The bottom line with something like this is you never know unless you ask. You can assume they would say one thing or another, but until you ask you never really know what someone is going to say. What is the worst that is going happen? They would say no. You are still not out anything more then the already agreed upon price. No gain, but no less either. For electricity, does your business have any windows? Are you adequately using your daylight instead of turning on lights and wasting electricity and money? Just an idea that may only save you a few bucks, but take those few bucks throughout the year and you may have just given yourself a couple extra hundred dollars in profit.

Have you thought about partnering with another business in some way? One of my favorite stories about partnering involves one of my favorite places to visit, which is Dave and Busters. If you have not been to one before, imagine an upscale video arcade with fine dining, pool tables, and arcade games. The business actually started as two separate businesses across the street from each other. One was the restaurant and bar with the other being the adult version of an arcade place. Both owners often saw people going from place to place, back and forth. One day they actually got together and planned to combine their businesses and now we have what is known as Dave and Busters. Is there a business around yours that would compliment it? Do not be afraid to approach other businesses in your area to setup something like a loyalty discount card or some sort of perk for shopping at both places. What is the worst that will happen? You guessed it, they would say no. You would not gain anything, but you would not lose anything either.

There are plenty of other ways to be creative in your business, but it is up to you to put them into action because you are the big boss man now. So no excuses, just personal blame. Think about some creative approaches you might be able to take when you begin your journey.

Lesson 26: Getting Out

So now that you have had your fun or pain of running your dream, it may be time to start planning your exit strategy. This can come in many shapes and forms, but the one thing that you need to keep in mind and remember through this last process is that businesses are not sold overnight, so it is NEVER to early to start looking ahead, even 5-10 years down the road or even if you are just thinking about it. It is always a good idea to have your affairs in order.

In that sense, you can almost think about selling your business as you would your own funeral. Almost all of us alive have at least some certain wishes or demands of what be done when it is our time. If you have planned accordingly, you may even have a little booklet or at least a letter explaining what your wishes are and everything that needs to be done when your time comes. This is what some refer to as a Legacy Drawer. I have no idea why it is called a drawer; my only guess is that the creator of such an idea kept this stuff in a specific drawer labeled UPON DEATH or something similar like that. In any case though, it is a place to write down everything that someone would need to know to make sure all of your affairs are in order. If you were to die tonight, would anyone be able to run your business effectively? Do they know all the little tidbits of information, passwords, and other junk that you have spent probably an entire lifetime learning about your business? It is never too early to start thinking about this type of stuff. If you are in my shoes, you probably would have already setup your exit strategy when you were planning your grand opening.

In my eyes, a business is always for sale; for the right price. If your business is not, then we need to have another discussion about the purpose of your business. Please read chapter one again where it clearly states that the purpose of a business is to make money, period.

Just like I have stated multiple times throughout this book, there are plenty of resources available to you when you start this process. There are entire books dedicated to making this process as tedious and stressful as you want it to be. I try to keep things simple with three easy rules when looking at selling a business.

The first is to set a clear objective of what you want from the deal. Most of the time this just comes down to a certain dollar amount you have in your mind. Have in your mind what you truly would accept as an offer and what you would feel comfortable with. Having unrealistic expectations is something that everyone has in their lives. If I met my expectation I would have been a rock star after college and be living in a 10-bedroom mansion right now. Life has a way of creating its own reality for you though, so this leads me into rule number two.

The second rule is to seek the advice of experience and trusted counsel. If you were trying to sell your house would you not call a real estate agent to help you? They deal with buying and selling homes every day as well as the experience they have to be able to tell you honestly and from an outside opinion what your business may be worth. Expect their final number to be less then what you think. It is nothing new that business owners over-value what their business is worth. It happens every day and probably to the company you work for as well. Trust the professionals with what their advice is and do not be afraid to get at least three opinions on what your business may be worth. The attention to detail in this rule is crucial to help show potential buyers what professionals think of your business and will help you at the bargaining table when a buyer low-balls you on their initial offer.

The last and most important rule in trying to sell your business was mentioned back many chapters ago when I discussed selling. Look at your business from the buyer's point of view. Ask yourself what questions they are going to come up with. Make sure you have simple and quick answers for them ready to go. You must be able to put yourself in the buyer's shoes and figure out what they want out of the deal. Why are they buying your business? Why should they purchase your business? What is in it for them? These may seem like simple questions and answers, but they are questions that come up time and time again when two parties start discussions on the purchase of a business.

One of the most important sets of documents to have prepared, clean, and ready for review are financial documents. Keeping good and clear records of your business will speak volumes to a potential buyer because it takes out the guesswork of what many small businesses fail at. An accurate balance sheet sends a clear message to potential buyers that you are organized and will establish a sense of trust with the buyer that a smooth transition of ownership will be possible when the deal is completed.

If I could give one piece of advice to businesses starting out it would be that you should never be going down with the ship. If you truly believe your business is failing or you see it as the right time to exit, do it. Do not hesitate in business because there are no points for second place. Just like selling a house, be careful about how you word why you are selling.

If you are selling a house, you are not going to tell a potential buyer that you are selling it because it is too small for you or your neighbor's house was just broken into. You would probably say something like you are moving closer to work or close to family. Am I telling you to lie? Possibly, but as long as you are not purposely hiding something from the potential buyer you should not have anything to worry about. It is their due diligence to make sure financials are in order, leases if required are up to date, and equipment is in good shape. This is all their due diligence. It may be your job to have a couple experts come out and give you an honest opinion of what your business is worth, like rule two suggests, but it is their duty as a potential buyer to do their own research.

Lesson 27: The End

Before I started writing this book many people asked me why I was writing a book. During the process, just as many people asked me why I was writing a book. All the same questions, what is it about, why are you writing it, what are you hoping to accomplish. My answer at the time was I do not know. I am just going to start writing and see where it takes me. I had a rough idea of specific topics I wanted to cover. Some chapters were obviously more in depth then others for a multitude of reasons. I guess I just had something I wanted to say in the matter.

It was a great experience writing the book and I enjoyed literally every minute, something I would probably never have thought I would say when I took on this task. I can now officially say I am an author, of some sort. I cannot think about when or where you may be reading this as it may be a week after it is published or it may be 75 years into the future and you came across it in a used book store or from a friend or family member.

Either and any way, it does not matter to me. I went into this with no expectations and no other goal other than finishing and having a published book. My only hope was that you enjoyed reading it and hopefully you learned and can take away at least one thing from this book whether it is negative or positive.

If I am still alive when you read this, please check out my website and let me know what you think of the book. www.brownconsultingwork.com

I hope you have a wonderful rest of the day and I wish you all the best and luck in the world if you decide to take that next huge step into starting your own business.

~Matthew Brown

www.ingramcontent.com/pod-product-compliance
Lightning Source LLC
Chambersburg PA
CBHW032005190326
41520CB00007B/362

* 9 7 8 0 9 8 3 2 5 9 3 9 8 *